Publishing
Years

Also by P. Anna Johnson

Australia Years:
The Life of a Nuclear Migrant

Publishing Years

The Story of a Small Press

by

P. Anna Johnson

Thirteenth Street Press
Portland, Oregon
www.pannajohnson.com

Interior Design by Slaven Kovačević

Library of Congress Control Number: 2020907087

Edition ISBNs:
Softcover 978-1-7349329-0-4
EBook 978-1-7349329-1-1

FIRST EDITION

Printed in the United States of America

For Nico, James and Penelope
(my grandchildren)

Acknowledgements

With heartfelt thanks to Sigrid, Kellenter, Sally Williams and Claudine Paris, members of my writing group for their patience and invaluable suggestions. Thank you to Gail Peck for explaining the technical aspects of book design prior to when we were using computers. Thank you Susan Stoner, Pat Andrus and Shakurra Amatulla for reading this manuscript, for your suggestions, and for urging me along until this book is becoming a reality. Thank you to my friends and family for all of your encouragement.

Table of Contents

Preface

Never in my wildest dreams did it ever occur to me that I might someday become a publisher. I was happy being an artist potter. But life takes its own course and change occurs if you allow it to. This is the story of how Open Hand Publishing Inc. came into existence and of the many people who played a role in its development.

I founded Open Hand in 1981 with the objective of promoting greater understanding and harmony among people of diverse heritages. It was at a time when white people and people of color lived, for the most part, in separate worlds in spite of it having been almost two decades since the passing of the 1964 Civil Rights Act; many women had come to the realization they were equal to men and were demanding their equal rights and an end to the glass ceiling; technology was progressing at such a fast pace we could scarcely keep up with it.

This book is a tribute to the many people who helped in so many ways to make Open Hand possible. I want my grandchildren, as they go about making their way in life, to know something about the heritage from which they come.

1.

An Accidental Profession

My marriage had recently ended and I was very much at loose ends in 1978, after having returned to the United States from Australia where I had lived for the previous 17 years. I bought a pleasant house on Seattle's Capitol Hill where I lived with my two sons; Arlo, age eight, and Jorma, age six. I wanted to launch myself into a new life and a new career but could not envision what that might be. I had been an artist potter in Sydney, working contentedly with clay, water and fire.

The transition from potter to publisher did not occur overnight. The seventeen years I had lived in Australia was such an important and interesting period that I started writing a book about them. So much has been written and sung about immigrants coming to the United States. I wanted to share my experience of having exited this country to become a migrant in another land. As I wrote I began investigating how to go about getting published. I read about self-publishing and the idea of publishing my own book seemed like an attractive possibility.

Two other things were going on in my life:

First, I was volunteering with Crabshell Alliance, an anti-nuclear organization in Seattle. Our primary objective was to close down the reactors operating in the Pacific Northwest. This was just after the Three Mile Island nuclear accident on March 28, 1979 that resulted in the release of radioactive gasses and radioactive iodine into the environment and radioactive wastewater into the Susquehanna River in Pennsylvania. There was a public outcry, throughout the United States, over the safety of nuclear power. In addition to Crabshell's monthly newspaper, we saw a need for a newsletter as a vehicle for getting information out quickly. I enrolled in a course in newsletter production at the University of Washington. Using techniques learned in that course, I created the *Crabshell Brief*. Through Crabshell Alliance I came into contact with the Workshop Printers, a printing collective in Seattle.

Second, although I was living in Seattle a large part of my heart was in Washington, DC with a man whom I had dated when I was a college student. His name was James Forman and we were resuming a relationship that had begun in 1957 when I was a sophomore majoring in philosophy at Colby College in Maine and Jim was a graduate student in the Africana Studies Program at Boston University. We met at a conference on disarmament held on the Harvard Campus, then spent the summer together in Chicago, Jim's hometown. I was enrolled in German language classes at the University of Chicago in preparation for spending my junior year abroad at the Albert Schweitzer College in Switzerland. After the first couple of weeks I spent increasingly more time with Jim, eventually giving up on attending classes altogether. There was some discussion about Jim coming to Switzerland too, but that didn't happen and we broke up while I was in Europe.

In 1961, after graduating from college then working for a year as a diagnostic counselor at the Boston Center for Blind Children, I married and moved to Sydney, Australia. About a year later, while sitting in our flat in Sydney reading *Time* magazine, I happened across a picture and an article about Jim. That is how I became aware of the

Student Nonviolent Coordinating Committee (SNCC) and that Jim was the Executive Secretary and one of the foremost leaders of the civil rights movement.

Two decades passed during which time Jim wrote two books that were published by major publishing companies; **Sammy Younge, Jr.: The First College Student to Die in the Black Liberation Movement** was published by Grove Press in 1968. **The Making of Black Revolutionaries**, published by Macmillan in 1972, was both an autobiography and an historical analysis of SNCC. It was the first book about the civil rights movement written by someone who was enmeshed in it. In 1980, for a master's degree thesis at Cornell, he was writing *Self-Determination: An Examination of the Question and its Application to the African-American People.*

I had told Jim about Seattle's Workshop Printers. He asked me if I would talk with them about printing his thesis. I took up the challenge. After returning to Seattle I phoned Danny Zucker, a co-op member at Workshop Printers. Danny liked the project and agreed to design a cover and the page-layout of *Self-Determination: An Examination of the Question and its Application to the African-American People.* I thought the title should be shortened to *Self-Determination and the African-American People.* Although Jim did not like this idea, he reluctantly agreed to it.

My original intent was simply to get the thesis printed. As the project progressed, Danny asked me to get an ISBN and a registration number from the Library of Congress. I had no idea what an ISBN was. During that conversation, or perhaps as I was walking back to my car, it dawned on me that I was publishing a book. I must be a publisher. I was assuming responsibility that required decision-making as well as financial investment. I began to envision this as a long-term venture with many more books to follow. Publishing was the answer to my search for a meaningful

3

career, and a way I could engage in helping to bring an end to racism. My objective was to publish books that would promote understanding between people of different races and cultures that would lead to positive social change.

The new publishing company needed a name. Some names up for consideration were "Equality Publishing" or "Harmony Press." I decided on Open Hand Publishing, the open hand being a symbol of acceptance, friendship, and sharing. Once I had a name, I went to a lawyer and had the company incorporated. I had no office so I used a private mailing service in downtown Seattle. Open Hand's first address was

Open Hand Publishing Inc.
5 Securities Building
1904 Third Avenue
Seattle, Washington 98101.

There was no roadmap to becoming a publisher. I did no research on the subject, but just made it up as I went along. I learned that ISBNs were issued by the R.R. Bowker Company and that the acronym stood for *international standard book number*. In their response to my request for an ISBN, they sent me a form that I filled out and returned along with a 50-dollar filing fee. For this, Open Hand was issued a list of 100 ISBN numbers the first of which, 0-940880-00-8, I used on Open Hand's first book, a paperback edition of **Self-Determination and the African American People** by James Forman. Each part of the ISBN has a meaning. The first "0" indicates the language in which the book is written with "0" being English. The second group in the sequence "940880" is the number assigned to the publishing company and the third, in this case, "00" is the number of this edition of the book. If a new edition is published it will receive a new ISBN number. The final single digit number is a mathematically calculated code to assure that the rest of the ISBN is recorded accurately. Every book published by Open Hand was issued the subsequent number and registered with R.R. Bowker with information they used when including the book in their listing of **Books in Print.**

Each book was also issued a number by the cataloging division of the Library of Congress. Based upon the subject matter of the book they determined the Library of Congress number and wrote a brief description to be included on the copyright page. They required that two copies of each new book be sent to them using a brilliant orange address label.

The copyright division of the Library of Congress also requires that two copies of each new book also be sent to them. This policy was established by Ainsworth Rand Spofford, the Librarian of Congress appointed by Abraham Lincoln, who recognized the value of such a collection. In 1870 a law was passed by Congress that read, " 'All records and other things relating to copyrights and required by law to be preserved, shall be under the control of the Librarian of Congress.' Anyone claiming a copyright on any book, map, chart, dramatic or musical composition, engraving, cut print, or photograph or negative thereof must send two copies to the Librarian within 10 days of its publication." (Goodrum, Charles A.: p. 25, *Treasures of the Library of Congress.* New York: Harry N. Abrams, Inc., 1991.)

◊ ◊ ◊

When I met Danny Zucker again in the cafe in the basement of the Elliott Bay Book Company to discuss plans for the paperback cover of **Self-Determination and the African-American People,** he said to me, "We need a quote for the back cover." Having read Howard Zinn's book, **SNCC**

The New Abolitionists, I thought that Zinn would be a good person to ask. I made a trip to the Seattle Public Library to find his address, and wrote to him at the department of political science at Boston University. After having received his reply that he would be happy to comment on **Self-Determination and the African American People**, I sent him a copy of the manuscript. Within a short time, a letter arrived from Howard Zinn with the following quote:

"James Forman's book is the first thorough examination I have seen of the important issue of Self-determination for African-Americans. He does an excellent history of the Communist Party's treatment of this question, and makes a forceful, provocative statement of his own. It should lead to an important discussion of the place of Afro-Americans in American society."

(This letter is in The James Forman Collection at the Library of Congress.)

Corresponding with a famous person pushed me out of my comfort zone, but I demonstrated to myself that I could do it.

My only previous publishing experience had been putting out the "Crabshell Brief" a monthly newsletter for the Crabshell Alliance. My children, Arlo and Jorma, were usually around and involved with work on the newsletter. So, for them, my publishing a book did not seem like a huge leap. Children in Jorma's third grade class were creating books. For a school assignment, Jorma wrote and illustrated The Little Bitty Snake, a fanciful story about the journey of a snake to an island where it encounters an ant. It deals with the struggle for survival as seen through the eyes of a child. At school it was turned into a bound book with a cardboard cover. Jorma begged me to publish his book. I had recently seen another book that had been written by a child and I thought that was an excellent way to empower children. I decided to publish the **Little Bitty Snake** in three bilingual editions, English/Spanish, English/French and English/Japanese. This was intended to be the first in a line of books written by children. Again, I turned to Danny Zucker and Workshop Printers for help in designing and printing **The Little Bitty Snake**.

Generally, a publisher's responsibilities are to find manuscripts, negotiate contracts with authors, oversee the editing and design of the books and covers, organize the promotional work, then distribute the books, keep track of all expenses and income from sales, and pay the author a royalty. Publishers do not usually print books. They get bids from several printers then select one for the job.

I knew as little about selling books as I did about producing them. Shortly after the entire print run of 2,500 copies of **Self-Determination and the African-American People** was delivered to the basement of my home on Seattle's Capitol Hill, I took one copy and drove about four miles to the University of Washington Bookstore. Fortuitously, the clerk I happened to speak with was, the bookstore's buyer, Marilyn Dahl. I hoped she would not notice my nervousness as I told her I was starting a new publishing company, handed her a copy of **Self-Determination**, and asked if she would like to purchase copies for the bookstore.

Taking the book into her hands she looked carefully at the cover, then the index. I assumed she was familiar with Jim's previous books, **The Making of Black Revolutionaries** and **Sammy Younge, Jr.: The First Black Student to Die in the Civil Rights Movement**. After leafing through the pages for about 40 seconds, she looked up at me and said, "I'll take 25 copies." At that moment, I thought selling books was going to be easy.

Next came a lesson in delivery. I went home, gathered together 25 copies of the book, then drove immediately back to the bookstore with the unwrapped books. The buyer was still in the same isle. She told me that I needed to take the books to "the second floor" and explained how to get there. The clerk who met me in "receiving" asked, "Where is the invoice?

"Invoice? I'm sorry, I don't have one."

The clerk called over the head of the receiving department. Instantly recognizing what a novice I was, this kind man gave me a 101 course in accounting that took about ten minutes. He guided me down two flights of stairs to the basement of the building where office supplies were sold. There he patiently showed me a double entry invoice book and carefully explained how to fill out an invoice, with one copy for the customer and one copy for myself. Picking up a sharp object that looked like a knitting needle mounted on a block of wood, he said, "Keep your copy and put it on this spindle." I bought an invoice book and a spindle on which to place the invoice for the first sale for the business to which I would devote the next 20 years of my life. I continued using the spindle for about the next three years, at which time I began using a computer for doing accounting.

2.

Washington, DC

1982 - 1986

On Memorial Day 1982, I set out from Seattle in my little blue Honda Civic hatchback to take up residence in Washington, DC. Jim and I had decided to renew an old dream and attempt to build our lives together. The tragedy of my life was that I was forced to leave Arlo and Jorma behind with their father. As a part of a custody dispute a psychiatrist and a social worker interviewed each of us. My lawyer explained to me that the judge usually follows their recommendation. The psychiatrist, while sitting in my living room, said to me, "I will recommend that Arlo and Jorma be placed in your custody." She paused then added, "... unless I find a skeleton in your closet." I felt jubilant as I thought I had no skeletons.

However, after my former husband was told by the same psychiatrist that she was going to recommend awarding custody to me, he told her that I was moving to DC to be with a black man. Until then, throughout the custody pro-ceedings, no one had questioned why I wanted to move to DC. After her discussion with my former husband, the psy-chiatrist called me into her office and cross-examined me about my reasons for wanting to move to DC. She specifi-cally asked me many questions about Jim who was a public figure and with whom she seemed familiar.

There was dead silence and disbelief in the courtroom when the judge announced that he was awarding custody to my former husband. At that moment my world fell apart and I could not imagine that I would ever recover. That was the worst day of my life, by far. I would not have considered a move across the country had I thought my children could not come with me.

But, I had to go on living and ultimately I decided to move to DC even though it would mean being separated from my children for much of the year. They would spend summers and Christmas vacations with me. Having a long continuous time together would be better than having the children split each week between my house and their father's house.

When I left Seattle early in the morning on Memorial Day 1982, my little Honda Civic was packed to the gills. En route, I stopped in Salt Lake City to visit my dear friend Della Piana, a close friend ever since we were co-workers at the Boston Center for Blind Children, before I moved to Australia. I then headed northeast to visit John Johnson (no relation) who had been a Fulbright scholar doing research at Sydney University. John had lived with us in Sydney for the six months prior to Jorma's birth.

After I arrived in Washington, Jim and I searched for a house with plenty of room for the children. We soon found a 3-bedroom house on Capitol Hill, 246 9th Street, NE. The day before Arlo and Jorma arrived for the summer Jim and I moved furniture from Jim's apartment. The moving van bringing my furniture and belongings from Seattle did not arrive for another couple of weeks.

◊ ◊ ◊

I had been active in the peace movement in Seattle, and in Boston before having moved to Australia. I carried with me to DC an invitation to a reception honoring Dr. Benjamin

Spock to be held by the SANE Committee of Nuclear Dis-armament. The SANE office was within a few blocks of my new home, so Jim and I walked to the reception.

I was excited about the prospect of meeting the famous baby doctor whose advice I, like millions of other new mothers, relied upon heavily those first few months after my first baby was born. I was not expecting to actually talk with him. But when Dr. Spock saw Jim, he came to greet us and hugged Jim like they were old friends - which they were. This was the first occasion where I saw Jim as a public persona. People recognize, knew, respected, and even loved him as a civil rights leader. I had never known him in that capacity. Later on in the evening, I was completely surprised and overcome when Dr. Spock, as he was passing by me, leaned over and kissed me on the cheek. That party marked the beginning of life in DC, a city filled with people that shape the way the world moves. I looked forward to being a part of a community making positive change.

Even before my furniture arrived, we had a houseg-uest. Jim had invited Josie Fanon, widow of Frantz Fanon, to come from her home in Paris to help him translate **Self-Determination** into French. For many years Jim had been working on a manuscript about Frantz Fanon whose writings about colonialism and racism, (especially his book **The Wretched of the Earth**) had inspired freedom fighters throughout the world. Jim traveled to Martinique in the winter of 1969-70 to interview Fanon's mother, and then to Paris where he interviewed and became friends with Fanon's widow.

Josie stayed at our house for a few days, before moving into an apartment in SE. Jim, who was fluent in French, and Josie enjoyed playing scrabble in French. Arlo, Jorma, Josie, Jim and I played the game together in English. Being in Washington was difficult for her as it brought back memories of when her husband was seeking treatment for advanced cancer in adjacent Bethesda, Maryland. He died there in 1961. Josie and Jim worked on the manuscript every day in Washington's sultry heat. Each day in the late afternoon, we would all go for a swim in an outdoor pool. It was the perfect way to cool down. Swimming was very important to Jim who was proud of his lifesaver certificate. He had not learned to swim until after he was well into adulthood and after laws has been passed requiring that public swimming pools be desegregated.

◊ ◊ ◊

In the 1980s Washington's population was about 70 percent black and it was sometimes referred to as "chocolate city". Being in the minority was a new experience for me. There were black and white areas of town, and where we lived was mixed. It seemed to me that the folks I saw on my block, in the supermarket, in the parks and on the busses got along well. Washington's first black mayor Marion Barry had been mayor of Washington, DC for four years. Before coming to Washington in 1964, he had been the first chairman of the Student Non-Violent Coordinating Committee (SNCC). SNCC's head office was in Atlanta and as the organization grew, offices were established in cities all across the country. As executive secretary of SNCC, Jim sent Marion to Washington to open SNCC's DC office. There were many other SNCC people who were officials in the DC government.

◊ ◊ ◊

We spent the first two weeks of August on Cape Cod with both Jim's and my children; the first time we had all come together. For a brief moment it felt like we were a family. We went to the beach, played softball and hide-and-seek, shopped at the grocery store and prepared meals. On the last morning the kids began to argue as we gave the house a final cleaning and packed our belongings into Jim's station wagon. It was a terrible note to leave on, until Jim said something that relieved the tension and put everyone at ease. The ability to find a resolution to a difficult situation was part of his genius.

◊ ◊ ◊

Not long after returning to DC from Cape Cod, on August 22, the day arrived when Arlo and Jorma had to leave for Seattle. I drove them to Dulles Airport. As I watched them disappear down the corridor towards the plane, it seemed as though my life was dropping away. To this day, when I am in an airport and see single parents saying goodbye to their young children, my heart breaks in two. Returning to the empty, silent house was unbearable. I managed to get through the night. In the coming days and weeks I focused my thoughts on the future and on learning about publishing.

Throughout the summer I visited several bookstores in DC and New York, just as I had done in Seattle. It came as a surprise that buyers in the larger bookstores were reluctant to place an order for an individual title. They were accustomed to dealing with a distributor who carried many titles. It was apparent from very early on that Open Hand was going to need a distributor. How I was going to find one was a mystery.

◊ ◊ ◊

Jim was very disciplined and intensely occupied all of the time with study, writing, and meetings. Apart from going to the swimming pool in the late afternoons, he allowed himself little time for relaxation. One day, when I was planting some petunias in the handkerchief size front yard, Jim objected saying, "That's a waste of your time." Something so natural to me was unfamiliar to him.

Although Jim seldom talked about it, I gradually came to learn about the extent to which the government, through the COINTEL program, had hounded him to the point of making life for him almost unbearable. Keeping him under surveillance for years was a tactic they had used to prevent him from carrying on with political organizing.

The Freedom of Information Act (FOIA) enabled Jim to acquire thousands of pages of documentation that the FBI and CIA had collected about his life and activities. These papers stood in about five stacks in the living room, each stack almost waist high. On many of the pages black ink made by a thick marker pen blocked out much of the typeface. On some of the pages, all of the type had been blacked out. It was the practice of the government to black out the names of operatives and anything else that might be revealed about their operations. All of this painful history was inescapable and very much in evidence in the living room. One might say, it provided a background to our lives.

Throughout the 1960s I had lived in Australia and I had not been a part of the Civil Rights Movement. Apart from what I had seen on television, I did not know what had happened during those years in the South. It was impossible for me to fully grasp what it meant to have been on the front lines of the Civil Rights Movement. Those were years of terrible, dangerous struggle during which time Jim's life was under constant threat. He had not come through that experience unscathed, and he was not the same person I knew earlier. We provided one another with a link to the past and I continued to view him as the youthful man I had known two decades earlier. But now, there was no one, including me, who could gain his trust. His suspicion of me would come out at the most unexpected times. We would be enjoying a quiet peaceful time after supper, playing music on the record player, maybe even dancing, and we would be about to go to bed when out of the blue he would accuse me of working for the CIA.

My heart was broken over and over again. As a way of protecting myself against repeated disappointment, I arranged to live nearby so I could always escape to my own space. Sometimes we did not see one another for weeks, or even months. But, we would inevitably make up at some point and the whole pattern would repeat itself. This went on for years.

Jim seldom spoke about the bizarre incidents of his life in the movement. He did say once that he had been approached by a young man with a gun who told him that he had been sent by the FBI to kill him, and that upon doing so the young man would be paid $300. When I asked, "What did you do?" Jim replied, "I told him it would be best for him to leave."

Although, of course, I knew that Jim was the leader of SNCC, I never knew what that entailed. Many years later, on the occasion of his 70th birthday celebration, Eleanor Holmes Norton said, "Jim was not only the person who kept the trains running on time. He built the trains." As Washington, DC's representative to the United States Congress, she entered this description into the Congressional Record.

Jim Forman was the Executive Director of the Student Nonviolent Coordinating Committee when it was at its best and at its height. This was the SNCC that pioneered the non- violent techniques of the sit-ins at segregated lunch counters; that organized the Mississippi Freedom Democratic Party that broke segregated national convention delegations in both parties; and that originated the

1964 Mississippi civil rights summer that brought an integrated army of students into the South to break open the worst and most dangerous areas. These historic achievements required more than young people who were willing to sit in, go to jail, or risk their lives. Jim did those and more. Jim was the sturdy hand at the helm who brought order out of movement chaos, kept everybody focused, and headed off trouble. I remember Jim as the forceful man in charge who was good at the whole range of human interactions. He could cajole, he could persuade, he could entice, and, if necessary, he would order.

SNCC was an extraordinary, collegial, decentralized movement organization. Its loose structure, youthful participants, and free spirits demanded a special leader. How fortunate our band of the young and foolish were. At the moment when we needed a leader who could hold us all together until the segregated south succumbed to the rule of law, we found one– James Forman.

◊ ◊ ◊

Jim and I found we got along better when we each had our own living space. I think it was because of our relationship before the civil rights movement that our love and respect for one another never ceased, even though living together was impossible. Jim was always passionate about life, about justice, about writing, or whatever he became involved in. He had maintained his charm and grace, but was no longer the relaxed person I had known two decades earlier. Years in the civil rights movement, which was a war zone, left him anxious, suspicious, and always on guard against attack. For example, he would not start the engine of his car without first checking under the hood to make sure no one had tampered with the wiring.

Also, my having money and Jim having none put a strain on the relationship. I paid for everything we did together and supported his non-profit organization, the *Unemployment and Poverty Action Committee* (UPAC). Soon after arriving in DC, Jim took me to the UPAC office, a spacious room on the third floor in the Methodist Building directly across the street from the Capitol Building and the Supreme Court. This location was most impressive. I was eager to be a part of a team of people working to create better conditions for poor people. When Jim asked me if I would be secretary of the organization, I gladly agreed. On UPAC stationary were the names of many eminent people on the Board of Directors and about 20 illustrious people, including James Baldwin and Harry Belafonte, who comprised the Board of Advisors. But, there were no meetings. Slowly I came to realize that there were no other people directly involved in decision-making or in the day to day running of UPAC. At first I was comfortable giving generously to the organization. Over the next year or so my doubts grew about whether it was a viable organization, until finally I withdrew from being secretary and no longer supported UPAC financially. Of course this was damaging to our relationship as Jim put his heart and soul into developing UPAC. I appreciated that he worked tirelessly to draw attention to the needs of poor people. What I could not accept about UPAC was that there were no other people involved in the daily working of the organization. I continued to support Jim personally.

Jim had an eclectic and fairly large record collection and occasionally we would dance to soft music in his apartment. Some of the old oak floorboards squeaked. Dancing together brought back memories of summer in Chicago all those years ago – before SNCC existed and before I moved to Australia.

Special favorites of Jim's were Nat King Cole, Nina Simone, and blues singer, Nancy Wilson. As years passed, we listened to music less frequently. I noticed that the record player was broken and I decided to give Jim a new one for Christmas. Christmases were special as both Jim's children and my children were with us for the holidays.

It was a shock when Jim rejected the record player because it was made in China. I didn't think about that when I bought it, even though I knew Jim had determined he would use only products made in the USA. He was very ridged about it and tried unsuccessfully to get me to agree to do the same. After that, the record collection remained untouched as there was never another record player in the apartment. This is not to say he was without music. He had a tape recorder, but it was not the same.

◊ ◊ ◊

Open Hand was possible because of an inheritance I had received from my parents. Learning how to manage my inheritance involved a steep learning curve. My first serious questioning concerning money occurred when I was about twelve years old. It was a Sunday morning and I was in the Saint Paul's Methodist Church in Niagara Falls, New York where I grew up. Rev. Redmond, the minister, was giving a sermon based upon the biblical passage about a camel going through the eye of a needle.

> And again I say unto you, It is easier for a camel
> to go through the eye of a needle, than for a rich man
> to enter into the kingdom of God.
> King James Bible Matthew19:24.

I tried to imagine such a thing and decided it was impossible. There is no way a camel could go through the

18

eye of a needle. Perhaps it was at this point that I decided it is not a good thing to be a rich person. Thereafter, I felt guilty about enjoying the privileges of wealth. In retrospect, one privilege I am happy to have benefited from was having received an excellent education.

While in college, I longed for the time when I would be able to support myself and no longer be dependent upon my parents. In my senior year, my professors in the department of philosophy and religion told me that with my interest in ethics and justice, I would be a good candidate for Harvard Divinity School. When they advised me to apply for graduate studies there, I rejected the idea outright because I wanted to get a job and become financially independent. It never occurred to me that it would be possible to do both.

In the fall of 1960, after graduation from college, I moved to Boston and within a week found employment as a diagnostic counselor at the Boston Center for Blind Children. The pay was 47 dollars per week. Rent on my apartment was 32 dollars per month. Come spring of 1961, I had saved 1,000 dollars and felt confident that this was sufficient to allow me to quit my job and devote my time to other interests.

That fall I married Robert Rodieck, a graduate student in electrical engineering at Massachusetts Institute of Technology (MIT) and we sailed on a freighter across the Pacific to Australia. I knew that Jim had married and that he was living in the South. Bob and I arrived in Sydney with 300 dollars between us. We were totally confident that we would be able to find jobs. Finding employment was easy in a country where the unemployment rate was below one percent. The day after we arrived, Bob began working as a temporary lecturer in the physiology department at the University of Sydney. Within a few weeks, I began teaching modern dance part-time at Penshurst Girls' High School. The following year, I worked full-time as a research assistant in the economics department at the University of Sydney where I calculated figures about Australia's unemployment rate. For the next 15 years, we lived comfortably, but modestly. We were never troubled by having either too little or too much money.

In 1968, Bob and I returned to the United States on sabbatical leave. While visiting my parents in Niagara Falls, Mother handed me a sheaf of papers with little explanation as to what they were. I sat down at my old desk, where I had done my high school homework, and tried to make sense of what I had been given. It wasn't exactly a will, but was more like a financial statement. I had never seen a financial statement before. Not understanding it, I handed it over to Bob, who was very adept at numbers, saying, "What do you make of this?"

After studying the document for 5 or 10 minutes, he said, "It means you will inherit....." and then he said some number that I couldn't comprehend. To this day, I have no idea what it was. Some hundreds of thousands of dollars, or perhaps even a million or more. I don't know. I replied, "Really?" and he said something like, "Yes. That's what it says." I think he was displeased by this turn of events. Perhaps he felt it negated his power. In any event, from that day on, we said no more about it. It seemed unreal.

We returned to Sydney in the spring of 1969; Arlo was born on November 16th, and Jorma was born on January 10, 1972. It must have been around 1974 that envelopes from my parents' building company began arriving at irregular and unpredictable intervals. In each one was a check for around 500 dollars. My parents had never given us any money before. Mother never said anything about it in her frequent letters. It was strange. We bought some furniture.

I came to understand that my parents were divesting themselves of their wealth, and that my siblings and I were the beneficiaries. One day a document arrived in the mail with instructions to sign it. Were I to do so, it would have given power of attorney to a brother who I did not think held my interest at heart. I wrote back saying, "No. Any documents that need my signature should be sent to me." My father was not accustomed to "no" for an answer from anyone, least of all from me. I was astounded when I started receiving phone calls from various members of the family who my parents thought might be able to influence me. Never in the 15 years I had been living in Australia had I received a phone call from anyone in the family, not even when my children were born. So I knew how important this was to my parents. They were horrified when I suggested I could hire a lawyer in Niagara Falls to act as my power of attorney. "No. We don't want any damn lawyer knowing about our business." Finally, they agreed.

The controversy with my family was a disturbance in my otherwise tranquil life in Sydney. But, life went on. After the children began going to school, I resumed the career I had been building as a studio potter. I sold my pottery at Paddington Market, a large craft bazaar. I put no prices on my work. When someone picked up a pot and asked, "How much does it cost?" I replied, "Whatever you would like to pay." Most customers wanted to pay a fair price, and some, who could afford to, overpaid me, compensating for those who under paid. Over time it worked out well.

◊　◊　◊

My father died in April 1980 and my mother died in May 1981. By this time I was divorced and living in Seattle, Washington. It took a few years for their estates to be resolved and by that time I had moved to Washington, DC where, at first, I used The Unemployment & Poverty Action Committee in the Methodist Building; 120 Maryland Avenue NE as my mailing address. Within days of my arrival in DC, dozens of thick envelopes bearing the return addresses of General Electric, Standard Oil, and the like, began filling the mailbox. In the envelopes were stock certificates. It was embarrassing, and Jim did not like it.

Here I was, a person who does not believe that large amounts of money should be passed from one generation to the next, wondering what to do with stock certificates inherited from my parents? It was all a strange and unknown world to me and I knew no one to whom I might turn to for advice. In an effort to help, Jim, with whom I was still living, arranged a meeting for me with his lawyer, Michael Standard, a partner in the New York law firm Rabinowitz, Boudin, Standard, Krinsky & Lieberman. The firm had been deeply involved in advising and representing activists in the civil rights movement and opponents to the Vietnam War. Jim and I drove to New York where we met with Michael Standard who advised me to begin by depositing all the stock certificates I had received in a safety deposit box in a bank. After our discussion, while Jim and Michael were engaged in a private conversation, Leonard Boudin showed me about his office. I felt that I was causing him to think of his daughter, Kathie, formerly a member of the Weather Underground, who was serving time in prison for her role in a Brinks robbery which had taken place in 1981 during which two police officers and a security guard were killed.

The next day, after returning to DC, I opened an account at a bank on Pennsylvania Avenue, a few blocks from my house. As more stock certificates from oil companies and large corporations arrived in the mail, I deposited them in the safe deposit box. It was uncomfortable having anything to do with these corporations, but I didn't know what else to do. If I were destined to have money, then I would put it to good use. My inheritance would make it possible to promote positive social change through Open Hand.

Whereas, part of my inheritance came in the form of stock certificates and money from my parents' life insurance, the bulk of it was in the form of stock in the family business, the Walter S. Johnson Building Company, Inc. My parents intended that the stock in this privately held corporation be divided evenly between their four children. My brother, Jack, was the president of the building company and also executor of my parents' wills. Jack, and his wife, Dorothy, were intent upon seeing to it that that my sister, Bess, my brother, Taylor, and I receive as little as possible. When it became clear that they regarded the building company as their own, to do with as they pleased, I contacted Don Lischer, a high school classmate of mine who was now a lawyer in Buffalo.

Even though philosophically I do not believe that fortunes should be passed from one generation to the next, I decided to fight for my inheritence and to use it to promote social justice. So, I set about taking legal action. I persuaded my sister to join me. Our lawyer told us that in order to build a strong case our other brother, Taylor, would need to join with us. Unfortunately, Taylor refused, saying his nerves couldn't take it. I had been warned by a lawyer who knew Jack personally, never to be alone with Jack – that he might do me physical harm.

The long and ugly legal battle, lasted over a year, and caused both Bess and me a great deal of emotional pain. In the end a settlemant was reached in which we each got about a half a million dollars, something like twenty percent of what we should have received. I continued living simply as I always had.

◊ ◊ ◊

George Washington University had just initiated the *Publishing Specialist Program*; graduate level classes on all aspects of publishing. It was the best place in the United

States to learn about publishing. I applied, was accepted, and began classes in September of 1982. There were about 50 men and women enrolled in the program, most of whom were employed full-time in some aspect of the publishing world; proofreaders, editors, graphic designers, etc. Many were from government offices. At first, I found it rather intimidating. One day I asked the student sitting next to me about what sort of work he did. I was astounded by his reply; "I am the head of printing and documents for the CIA and have about 60 people working under me."

I was surprised to learn that indexing is a profession, and that there were classes offered to prepare people to become certified indexers. I thought back to when an index was needed for Open Hand's first book, **Self-Determination and the African-American People**; and I just created one myself. I enjoyed doing it and it never occurred to me that I might not be doing it correctly.

The class *Fundamentals of Proofreading* covered every aspect of proofreading. I am forever grateful to my teachers for having introduced me to proofreading codes, and to Strunk and White's **The Elements of Style**, and **The Chicago Manual of Style**. Spending endless hours doing homework assignments in which long essays with complex sentence structures had to be unscrambled was a challenge I enjoyed.

My favorite class was *Tools and Techniques of Graphic Design*. It was still being taught as though computers had not yet been invented. Tools required for the class included a ruler, right angle triangle, compass to make circles, glue stick, rubber cement, waxer, bees wax, #2 pencils, HB pencils, two kinds of erasers, and a large brush to be used to clean up after you were through erasing. I loved the hands on work that reminded me of my pottery days.

Using my new tools and the new skills learned in this class, I created flyers for **Self-Determination**. I took them to bookstores all over the city, and handed them out at demonstrations, rallies, concerts, and wherever I thought people with an interest in civil rights and self-determination might gather. My quandary was that I did not have a distributor yet, and could not find one that was interested in a publisher with only two titles.

But word was getting around and orders for **Self-Determination** kept arriving in Open Hand's mailbox. I packaged the books, carried them to the post office, and mailed them. Mostly, they were orders for single copies. In November, I was delighted when I received an invitation to have a display at a media event at the Association for the Advancement of Negro History and Life, one of the places I had visited to promote **Self-Determination**. This was a great honor and I was amazed to have been invited. Guests at the event included James Baldwin. This was my first experience creating and minding a book display.

◊ ◊ ◊

It was easy to take care of any correspondence and conduct Open Hand business from my dining room table. I established a new mailing address at a mailing service near Eastern Market, within walking distance from my home on NE 9th Street.

Open Hand Publishing Inc.
210 Seventh Street, SE, Suite A24,
Washington, 20003

◊ ◊ ◊

Striving to enhance Open Hand's professional appearance I obtained an answering service. By dialing a code, I could turn the service on, at which point a receptionist would take messages as though she was my personal secretary.

Answering machines were not yet in common usage, and in any event, it was classy having a human being with a pleasant voice answer the phone.

Running the publishing company and taking classes still left me time to volunteer at the offices of the *Sane Committee for Nuclear Disarmament* and *Women Strike for Peace* (WSP), both within easy walking distance from my house. I learned how to lobby on Capitol Hill and frequently participated in demonstrations. I helped publish the monthly newsletter that was sent to several thousand subscribers all across the United States. As well as giving me a sense of purpose, this work brought me into contact with people with whom I became good friends.

◊ ◊ ◊

Technical problems that the typesetter was having with the production of **The Little Bitty Snake** had been resolved and each of the three language editions arrived. This delightful little book just about sold itself, and everyone I showed the book to wanted a copy. At that point I did not know about how important it is to promote a book in advance of its arrival, and I had done nothing.

Living within walking distance of the Library of Congress, I decided to hand- deliver two copies of each of the three language editions to the copyright department. The man at the desk was not particularly surprised until he looked at the form that included the year of birth of the author. After reading that the author was born in 1972, he made a quick calculation that told him the author was ten years old. The kindly man looked up and said, "My, these authors are getting younger and younger."

◊ ◊ ◊

At Thanksgiving I flew to Seattle where Arlo, Jorma, and I spent the holiday together in our house, which was rented to a friend. When I returned to DC, I took my cat, Chestnut, with me. He proved to be a very good companion in my too-large house.

◊ ◊ ◊

I was still questioning whether or not I wanted to be a publisher when I wrote in my journal:

December 10, 1982

> *Î have been grappling with the responsibility of Open Hand. In my earlier expectations for my life, I never anticipated becoming an administrator. I expected that I would work either alone (as was the case in the pottery) or in conjunction with others. Now I find myself in a situation where it will become increasingly necessary to hire others and to direct them in their work. I find the prospect of becoming "boss" rather frightening. I don't want to be in a position of directing others about what they should do. I enjoy "doing" more than "directing".*

When I expressed these thoughts to Jim, he suggested that I hire a manager to run Open Hand and do the art work myself.

Simply articulating and clarifying my doubts went a long way towards increasing my enthusiasm for the publishing company. Later the same day I wrote, *Open Hand needs an office, telephone, good electric typewriter, word processor or computer, and a photo copy machine, as well as office furniture, filing cabinets, etc.*

◊ ◊ ◊

When the children returned to Seattle after Christmas vacation the large empty house was again too quiet and dark, and I was despondent. Still a stranger in Washington, I felt lost and lacking in purpose and direction. The only thing to do was to throw all of my energy into the publishing classes at George Washington University. A lecture by Peter Givier from the *Association of American University Presses* (AAUP) struck a strong chord. The topic, *Publishing as an Accidental Profession*, made a great deal of sense. He explained that becoming a publisher is not something that one sets out to do. It is something that one falls into accidentally and there is no training. The only way to learn how to become a publisher is to do it. Hearing my situation described so precisely was a great relief.

I took a course in computing, but it was theoretical and there was not one computer in sight. I do not know why it was thought we had to know how computers work. That is like thinking that in order to drive a car one has to first understand motor mechanics.

The concept of a personal computer was unknown. Adam Osborne had just invented the first portable computer, and it was called the "Osborne." IBM would launch a portable personal computer in 1984, the "IBM 5155." In 1988, Compaq Computer would launch the first laptop PC. The first Apple Computer did not appear until 1989, and it was described as "luggable," not "laptop."

In keeping with the *Publishing Specialist Program's* objective of presenting a well-rounded overall view of the publishing process, there was a course in *Finances and Accounting*. It went far beyond my experience and comprehension. Like most small businesses at that time, I managed Open Hand's accounts with the use of a ledger book and hand-written spreadsheets. I knew that eventually I would have to learn to use a computer to do the accounting. How or when that might happen, I could not imagine.

Meetings of the *Washington Book Publisher's Association* were held on the second Wednesday of each month, on a rotating basis, at various institutions that had a publishing arm: *National Geographic Society, National Archives, Georgetown University, World Bank, National Academy of Science, etc.* Simply showing up and experiencing the environment was an education in itself.

In February 1983, I purchased Open Hand's first piece of equipment - a high quality *Xerox* copy machine that fit easily into the living room. Some months later I purchased a *Xerox Memorywriter;* an electric typewriter with three revolutionary features: a small pinwheel that could be slipped in and out to change font; the ability to cover over a typo with whiteout, and a 300-word memory. I used the new equipment to create promotional materials.

◊ ◊ ◊

Still uncertain about how much I wanted to be a publisher, I wrote in my journal:

June 10, 1983

> *Both my body and my mind seem to resist getting down to seriously working hard on Open Hand. I keep nourishing it along and dabbling in it. And this concerns me because I usually enjoy working hard on a project and watching it develop. Why then am I not working hard on Open Hand?*

> *Perhaps the reason is that fundamentally I am an artist and not a manager. I want to create things anew rather than handle what is already in existence. It can be argued that managing is a creative activity - that it is an "art". I think this is stretching a point. There can be creative and innovative*

*management, but that is not to say that management
is synonymous with creativity. In fact, the two func-
tions work in opposite ways. Management requires a
clear plan and getting down to brass tacks day after
day. In order to be creative, you have to be free to let
new ideas come pouring in. You have to take the roof
off.... even though it might mean letting the wind and
rain in. In management you need a good secure roof
so that the papers and organization won't be damaged in the storm.*

◊ ◊ ◊

Arlo and Jorma were with me for the summer, during which
time Arlo took a course in computing and Jorma joined a
soccer team. We made a leisurely trip north, first visiting my sister in Manhattan, then cousins in Rhode Island,
before heading up to Maine. The children returned to Seattle before the 20th anniversary celebration of the March on
Washington, which took place on August 27th.

September 1, 1983

> The March on Washington for jobs, Peace and
> Freedom was so big and so important it is almost
> impossible to express my feelings about it. For me it
> was a way of catching up with where I wanted to be
> twenty years ago. At last I am here and I am partici-
> pating. I marched with Women's Strike for Peace and
> gave out buttons saying "Self-Determination for the
> African-American People – UPAC."
>
> Three hundred thousand people were there on
> Saturday representing all of the issues: civil rights,
> labor, women, peace, environment, gays. We all stood
> together under the intense sun. Temperature was

30

in the 90s. One thinks about the excitement and the thrill of being there while the pain and difficulty that people go through to attend is often forgotten. The long long bus and car rides for many. The heat and dehydration that you experience, and the just plain sore feet. Most people didn't attend just for the "fun". They want something very very badly.

My friend, Barbara Brown, flew in all the way from Alaska for the March. Unaccustomed to Washington's sultry weather, she actually fainted as we were walking along the Mall. March organizers who were well prepared for such an emergency were immediately on hand with bottled water and she was quickly revived.

◊ ◊ ◊

In September 1983, many things happened all at once. I had spent the first year or so in DC acclimating myself, and now things were starting to move. Walking in Eastern Market, I noticed a FOR RENT sign in the second floor window above a florist shop. After inspecting it, I decided it would make an excellent office for Open Hand.

September 15, 1983

> *Found a wonderful place by Eastern Market for Open Hand's office. I'm delighted with the space and know I'll be able to work well there. - quiet and lots of light in an old brick building. For some reason the space reminds me of my pottery. This space would make a wonderful pottery instead of a publishing company. Things have been moving so slowly with the publishing company – but I'm determined to persevere. Things were slow with my pottery at first.*

31

Just as I was looking forward to having an office within walking distance from home, it came as a shock when the landlord of my house gave me notice that he was going to sell the house and I would have to move. I had first option to buy, but at that time I was not interested in purchasing a house in DC. I still owned my house in Seattle. I set out to find an apartment, preferably in NW to be near Jim. I dropped by *Food for Thought*, a funky restaurant on Connecticut Avenue, to have a look at their bulletin board. When I found a notice ROOMMATE WANTED FOR GROUP HOUSE ON HARVARD STREET NW, I decided there would be no harm in checking it out. With well- proportioned large gracious rooms, a living room featuring arched windows from floor to ceiling, and a graceful staircase, this was no ordinary house. I would have a bedroom, sitting room, and large bathroom to myself. The rest of the house, which included a back porch running the full width of the house on the second floor, would be shared with a young married couple, Danny and Gail Peck. Danny was a photographer and Gail was a graphic designer, and they each worked from home. They published a neighborhood newspaper, *The Columbia Road*. When they said they were agreeable to my living there, I lost no time in moving to 1650 Harvard Street NW.

That same week, I went to the annual Adams Morgan Street Fair where I met Shakurra Amatulla, an attractive energetic young woman who was selling a book she had self-published, **Get Your Money Honey,** about obtaining grant money. I could scarcely believe I had found another woman publisher. I introduced myself, told her about Open Hand, and invited her to visit my new office. She must have been the first visitor.

The office was bare bones – just a desk and chair, copy machine, typewriter, filing cabinet, and a brown rug that had been given to me by my next-door neighbor. Boxes of **Self-Determination** and **The Little Bitty Snake** were stored in a small room. It was a humble beginning, but I loved the space. It was an auspicious sign when, that first week in the new office, an order arrived from a wholesaler for 40 copies of **Self-Determination.**

Shakurra invited me to her house on 13th Street NW where I met her four daughters: Melissa, age 12; Khalilah, age 7; Naseema, age 2; and Aisha who was only one year old. I could not begin to imagine how Shakurra managed to raise her children, work full time as a legal secretary, as well as write and publish a book. She was a genius and a wonder. The two of us attended the *Third World Journalist's* conference held on the campus of Howard University. There I saw, but did not meet, a freelance publicist named Vicki L. Johnson who had her own company named *Communication Specialists of America*. Later in the week, I phoned and arranged to meet Vicki at my office. That was the beginning of a long collaboration in which we worked to promote Open Hand's books. It had taken a very long time to find the right person with whom to work. Vicki was a sophisticated, young black woman who dressed in a modest but elegant fashion. She, Jim, and I met to plan a campaign to promote **Self-Determination and the African American People**. Vicki introduced Jim and me to Barbara Cotell, a photographer who took photos of Jim to be included in press packets.

Christmas 1983 was the happiest time I could recall in many years. Jim, with his two sons, James and Chaka, joined Arlo, Jorma, and me in the large house where I was now living. On New Years Eve Jim and I, Arlo and Jorma joined Shakurra and her four girls for a relaxed easy time with much laughter at Shakurra's house. There was a surprise birthday cake for Jorma, whose birthday is on January 10th. The children and I were learning how to carry the burden of separation that existed in our lives.

After the children returned to Seattle, we kept in close touch by phone. In one of our conversations Arlo told me, "You must get at least a little inexpensive computer so that you can learn Basic." I did not know what Basic was, did not know how to operate a computer, and had no idea about how to go about shopping for one. My new friend, Shakurra and I commiserated about our lack of computer skills.

Working closely with Vicki Johnson, I learned a great deal about publicity. Things were falling into place quite naturally as Gail Peck became Open Hand's designer. We created press packets and sent out to radio and TV stations in DC and New York. It was a great thrill when they were met with a very positive response and Jim was invited to appear on the Fred Fisk Show, the Diane Rehm Show, WBAI, WUDC and many other radio and television stations in DC and New York. Things were turning around and Open Hand was at last beginning to function as a real publishing company.

The enthusiasm my new housemates, Danny and Gail Peck, had for Open Hand played a major role in its development. I literally had an "in house" designer, as the room in which Gail did graphic design was just down the hall from my bedroom. In those first months of our sharing the house, Gail created a logo and flyers that I took with me as I called on bookstore buyers.

Having attractive promotional material and a good mailing list was essential. In those days before the World Wide Web, that was the only way to get the word out. Paying for printing, mailing lists, and postage was all very expensive.

Gail was still doing graphic art the old way, without a computer. Recently, when I asked her to describe that process, she emailed back the following:

Hi Anna,

I definitely was not working on a computer at Harvard St. I'm sure the '86-'87 catalogs, covers, layouts were done manually. I didn't get my first Mac until the early 90s after moving to this house (late 1986). I briefly tried working on a windows-based PC with a program called Ventura Publisher but found it very cumbersome and soon went back to traditional methods.

The 80s was the transitional period from phototypesetting using photographic technology to generate galleys to digital typesetting using computer technology. In both cases, there were very distinct divisions of expertise and craftsmanship. The "writer" generated the copy (called "content" nowadays) on a typewriter. The "designer" submitted "comps" of design concepts, illustrated by hand. Once the final design was ready for production, the designer added typography notations to the manuscript (by hand with a pen/pencil) specifying the font, size, leading, column width, kerning etc, for all copy including headlines, subheads, text, cutlines (captions), folios (page numbers) basically any printed character. These "specs" were then sent out (usually by courier) to the "typesetter". The designer was never expected to type and typesetting was a highly regarded craft. The "magic" of converting the copy and all specifications to galleys was solely in the hands of the typesetter. The result was columns of black type on long sheets of slick white paper—galleys. Each galley was coated on the back with hot wax or rubber-cement glue. The galleys were then precisely trimmed with an Exacto® knife by the designer to fit the page and layout design. They were carefully applied to a "board" (heavy card stock) that included a drawn diagram of the page layout, trim-size, bleed, etc. It was important that a re-positionable medium like wax was used to allow for edits and design changes. These "art boards" or "mechanicals" included the copy, graphic elements and production instructions for printing. For photographs, a solid shape of black or orange or red, light-blocking film indicated the shape of the photograph and where the image should appear on the page. It was marked FPO (for position only) because the actual photograph was submitted separately (with careful coding so it would end up in the right place) and processed separately for placement by the production team in the "stripping" department at the printer. Each "board" represented a page or spread and had multiple layers to indicate different colors. Color was notated in the margins with color chips from the Pantone® system still in use today. Once approved and at the printer, the production team (called "strippers") prepared the mechanicals for the presses by converting them to a sheet of film for each color (very simply described). Press operators would then convert the film to metal plates for the presses. Stripping is among the highly specialized crafts, like typesetting, that are completely obsolete today and are managed digitally with computer software by graphic designers.

Anna, this is probably more than you need but I hope it helps. And please let me know if I can help you fill in anywhere else.

Love,
Gail

◊ ◊ ◊

My objective was to see Open Hand operating independently of my inheritance. I remained morally conflicted about being wealthy. When I learned there was to be a conference about issues related to inherited wealth, sponsored by an organization called *Common Capitol Support Fund*, I was eager to attend. George Pillsbury, a child of corporate America, was one of its founders. The conference dealt with the practical issues of how to invest in a socially responsible way, as well as the unique psychological problems of the wealthy. It was held at the Sheraton Hotel on Connecticut Avenue. To the ordinary person who struggles to meet the rent payments, or the mortgage, it would seem ridiculous that having excess money could be a problem. The normal thing to think would be, "I'd like a problem like that." But, along with inherited wealth often comes isolation and feelings of guilt. Frequently, people who are dependent upon inherited wealth feel inadequate, and are overcome with fear they will not be able to provide for themselves in the event that they somehow loose their money. This all too often leads to depression, alcoholism, and even suicide. Women who receive a large inheritance are sometimes prohibited, by the terms of the will, from determining how to spend it. I came to be friends with a woman, a gifted artist, who was in this situation. Continuously depressed, she eventually succeeded in committing suicide when she jumped off the San Francisco Bridge for the second time.

At this conference I met John Commack, a financial advisor who I felt I could trust. Shortly thereafter, I visited him at his office at Alexandra Armstrong Associates, located in a modern office building on Connecticut Avenue in downtown DC. At that time it was most exceptional for a man in the financial world to be employed by a woman. Alexandra Armstrong, a pioneer in financial planning, was the first certified financial planner in Washington, DC. John helped me to define my financial goals. I did not want to set up a retirement account. My top priority was to set aside funds to pay for half of Arlo and Jorma's college expenses. Their father and I had agreed earlier that we would each pay half. Over a period of time, my blue chip stock was sold and replaced by stock in socially responsible corporations, and mutual funds like the Calvert Fund. It was a great relief to have found someone I could trust to guide me on financial matters.

I was desperately in need of an accountant to set up a system for keeping track of my personal accounts, and to do my taxes. John Cammack put me in touch with Maureen Geimer. She never commented, but I imagine the disarray of my accounting must have horrified her. She brought it into good order and, with great patience, taught me how to keep track of income and expenditures using a red logbook.

I still strongly believe that our society would be stronger and people's lives happier if large amounts of money were not passed from one generation to the next. Instead, money would be returned to a common fund. Bob Moore, the owner of Bob's Red Mill, gave his 100 million dollar per year business to his employees. I heard him say in a radio interview, "Each thing I give away makes me feel better."

◊　◊　◊

I made a trip to Seattle for Arlo and Jorma's spring vacation. While there, I purchased a desktop computer, although I had no idea how to use it. I think it was an Osborne. Upon returning to my office, I placed it on a table and hoped that I could find someone to teach me how to use it. Even after taking private lessons on the use of *WordStar*, a word processor application that predated *WordPerfect*, I was fearful that if I touched a wrong key everything would break. When the children arrived for summer vacation, I gained confidence as I watched Arlo use the computer with no hesitation.

◊　◊　◊

My friend Shakurra and I did not know much about the *American Booksellers Association* convention, (ABA) being held that year in Washington, DC. We decided to go to the Convention Center and see what it was all about. We had our books with us, just in case, as we wandered about long aisles where publishers of all sizes and from all over the country displayed their new titles. We were overwhelmed by the size of the hall, the thousands of people milling about, bright lights, music, and books of every size and shape on any subject one might imagine. We two innocents glimpsed, for the first time, into the heart of the vast book industry where deals were being made and contracts signed. And because it was the afternoon of the last day of the event, some publishers were packing up and leaving early. Thinking it would be fun to display our books, we commandeered an empty booth, set our book out on the table, and stood beside them as though we were exhibitors. We were amazed when people assuming we belonged there asked us questions about the books. In years to come I would exhibit at the ABA, but it was probably never as much fun as that year.

◊ ◊ ◊

Even though I had received a positive response from bookstore buyers in Seattle, making the rounds of bookstores in Washington and New York was exceedingly challenging. This was big time and it took all the courage I could muster. I was met with a variety of responses. The buyer at Kramer Books simply was not interested. At Pyramid Bookstore, Hodari Abdul-Ali was not only eager to place an order, but in years to come he helped to promote all of the Forman books. Hodari, who understood the significance of Forman's work as civil rights leader and a political thinker and historian, helped to get the word out to political activists and librarians across the country.

◊ ◊ ◊

In the summer of 1984 Arlo, Jorma, and I made a return trip to Australia and for the eight weeks I was away, Shakurra Amatulla took care of Open Hand business by fulfilling orders and forwarding mail to me.

◊ ◊ ◊

Upon returning to DC in mid-August, things were beginning to fall into place. Open Hand now had an office, a designer, a public relations consultant, and an accountant. It was time to embark on new projects. I had received many requests for two books by James Forman that were out of print: **The Making of Black Revolutionaries** published by Macmillan in 1972 and **Sammy Younge, Jr.: The First Black College Student to Die in the Black Liberation Movement** published by Grove Press in 1968. I decided to republish both of them and began discussing plans for the design with Gail Peck. She was not yet using a computer so the books were done the old way with mechanicals. After Gail had made sketches of the covers, Jim came over to Gail's studio and joined in the discussions. Similarly, Jim joined in on Vicki Johnson's and my discussions about how best to promote the books. This was very much a team effort, and we all enjoyed working together.

The Making of Black Revolutionaries, is a large book of 568 pages written in two parts. Part I is an autobiography of Jim's early years. Part II begins in the spring of 1960, when about 300 students responded to a call from Ella Baker to attend *The Southwide Student Leadership Conference on Nonviolent Resistance to Segregation* held at Shaw University in Raleigh, North Carolina. The book is an account of what took place inside the *Student Nonviolent Coordinating Committee* from 1960 to the end of the decade. This very personal heartrending story was the first book to have been written by someone in the movement. When Macmillan published **The Making of Black Revolutionaries** in 1972, it received rave reviews:

> "We never really have understood that revolution—that era, those people, even ourselves during that horrible wonderful time—and this book helps us understand."
>
> —Life Magazine

> "An important documentary autobiography by a man who became one of the most important black leaders in the struggle for civil rights and freedom, this volume is moving, dramatic, at times almost overwhelming."
>
> —Library Journal

> "A searing, jolting document that will leave the reader full of that savage indignation that tears the heart."
>
> —New York Times

Open Hand published the first paperback edition of the book. Gail Peck designed a new cover and made all of the arrangements with the printer. To promote and celebrate the publication of **The Making of Black Revolutionaries** we held large receptions, first in Washington, DC, then in New York.

My commitment to publishing had become serious. Open Hand also published a new edition of **Sammy Younge Jr.: The First Black College Student to Die in the Black Liberation Movement**. This book was about the radicalization of a middle class black youth, Sammy Younge, a student at Tuskegee University who was shot down in a gas station in 1965 after refusing to use the black toilet. He had learned the lesson...that to live as a black man in white America, you have to be ready to die. Jim had met Sammy Younge on the Selma-to-Montgomery March in 1965. After Sammy's death, Jim decided to compile this book from the remembrances of Sammy's family, friends, and fellow SNCC workers.

When Grove Press published **Sammy Younge, Jr.** in 1968, it received excellent reviews:

" ...*a passionate indictment of the white racism that killed black student Sammy Younge* .... *A hard and affecting story.*"

–Library Journal

"*An important troubling book*. . . . *The author interviewed everyone who knew Sammy Younge, and their verbatim conversations describe not one youth but a seething segment of an entire population.*"

–Publishers' Weekly

There was a lot of work to be done at Open Hand, and I hired my first assistant, Linda Sanders, a young graduate of Howard University. She worked three days a week.

September 19, 1984

"*I have a part-time secretary now, Linda Sanders, and I think she is extremely capable. For me it is a major step to know how to have a secretary. Something that has become increasingly more necessary, but for which I am totally untrained and unprepared. I never went to "executive school" to learn how to supervise someone else. But I do know how to teach people ... so I can teach them and pay them at the same time."*

◊ ◊ ◊

Ronald Reagan became president in 1981 and was in the White House throughout the time I lived in Washington. When Walter Mondale ran against him in the 1984 election, I spent some time working on the campaign. After volunteering to answer the telephones, I was amazed when I was assigned to answer Senator Mondale's personal telephone in a campaign office on M Street. My job was to make sure no important incoming calls were lost while he was away campaigning. That was a thrill. Election day was cold and rainy. I was assigned to hold up a sign directing voters to the polling station in College Park, Maryland. That evening, Jim and I went to what we hoped would be a victory celebration at the Hilton Hotel. It was sad watching Mondale gave his concession speech in a large hall with few people in attendance.

◊ ◊ ◊

The injustice of apartheid had been a concern of mine since I was a teenager. I first became aware of apartheid in South Africa when, as a freshman in high school, I was cast as a black South African woman in the musical play **Lost in the Stars**, based on Alan Payton's famous novel, **Cry the Beloved Country**.

Pressure to end apartheid was growing within South Africa and from all over the world. Demonstrations took place every day from 4 to 6 pm in front of the South African embassy. A couple of days each week I joined the marchers chanting "Not one of us is free, 'til all of us are free." Among the first people to be arrested in front of the South African embassy were Marion Barry, Mayor of Washington, DC, Congressman John Conyers of Michigan and Bill Simons, vice-president of the American Federation of Teachers. I accompanied Jim when he went to the city jail to visit Congressman Conyers and ask him if there was anything we could get for him. Without much question we were escorted to the filthy cell where Congressman Conyers was being held. When we entered he stood up from where he had been sitting on an iron cot with no mattress.

People from all parts of the United States and all over the world flew to Washington to participate in anti-apartheid demonstrations being organized by *TransAfrica*. So many wanted to get arrested that it became necessary to book a date in advance. There were training sessions during which those who had volunteered to be arrested practiced for the event. Because the jail did not have the capacity to house all of the people who wanted to spend a night there, people were asked to opt for not staying in jail.

On the days when there were not so many visitors from afar, those of us who lived in DC filled in. I remember five of us walking towards the door of the embassy from where dozens of protesters were marching. When we reached a certain line drawn on the pavement, a policeman said to us, "If you go beyond this point you will be arrested." We crossed the line and stood just on the other side. Then, the policeman repeated three times, "If you remain on that side of the line you will be arrested." After the third time, we were arrested, handcuffed, escorted to a police car, and taken to the police station. Once there, we were fingerprinted, then released. No charges were pressed. The DC police, mostly black, were sympathetic to the cause of ending apartheid in South Africa.

Many movie stars came from Hollywood. Harry Belafonte was there one afternoon and Jim gave him a ride back to the airport. As the movement grew, demonstrations took place in cities around the globe and economic sanctions were placed on South Africa by organizations and governments from around the world. In 1990 the South African government lifted the ban on the African National Congress (ANC) and Nelson Mandela was freed after having spent 27 years in prison. In 1994 apartheid was dismantled and Mandela was elected President of South Africa.

◊ ◊ ◊

All my life I had been terrified of public speaking. It became increasingly clear that I would have to speak publicly, both in connection with the publishing company and for my work in the peace movement with Women Strike for Peace. Jim suggested that I enroll in a class in public speaking at the University of the District of Columbia (UDC). Eugene Wiggins was a marvelous teacher. By the end of the term, I felt confident about speaking publicly and I discovered that standing up and speaking before a large audience is enjoyable.

March 8, 1985

> *The class I'm taking in public speaking is going well. I gave a 10-minute speech on New Zealand's anti-nuclear policy and I received an A+. I'm jumping with joy. I would like to give that same speech many places. In order to become comfortable with public speaking I'm going to have to do more of it.*

Not long after I had completed the course in public speaking, I was invited to participate in a three-person panel on small press publishing at Howard University. One of the other panelists was Paul Coates, publisher of Black Classic Press. (He is the father of Ta-Nehisi Coates whose book **Between the World and Me** (2015) received rave

45

reviews.) After each panelist had given a presentation about their press, students were invited to ask questions. All was going well until I called upon a student who asked, "How do you finance your publishing company?" I was thrown for a loop because I did not want it known that I was the recipient of generous inheritance. I hedged and said something like, "Are you familiar with the proverbial *rich uncle?*

◊　◊　◊

Through Vicki Johnson, I met Lucyann Kerry, a publicist who lived in Manhattan. Lucyann thought that there was great potential for **Sammy Younge, Jr.** to be made into a movie and she began working to that end. She also worked with Vicki Johnson and me on two major events, one in Washington and one in New York, celebrating the publication of **The Making of Black Revolutionaries** as well as introducing Open Hand to the world.

I needed someone to be master of ceremonies at the reception in Washington. Jim suggested I ask E. Ethelbert Miller, director of the Howard University Afro-American Resource Center. He was also director of the Ascension Poetry Reading Series, one of the oldest literary series in Washington. I made an appointment and, within a few days, made my way to the Howard campus to meet with him. His office was on the third floor of the Founders Library, the large red brick building with a white dome that dominated the campus. Once inside, I made my way, following the directions I was given, up stairways, through endless stacks, along corridors, through narrow passageways until, eventually I found the man I was searching for. Seated at a huge old desk, he was surrounded by books and papers. Ethelbert, warm and welcoming, greeted me with a huge smile and asked what he might do to help me. He was much younger than I had expected. I explained about Open Hand and that there would be a reception to celebrate the publication of a new paperback edition of **The Making of Black Revolutionaries**. Ethelbert was more than happy to be MC at the reception set for July 23rd. It was held at the Mott House, a beautiful mansion belonging to the Mott family (Mott apple sauce), located across the street from the Capitol Building and the Supreme Court. The Mott Family makes the mansion available to progressive causes.

July 25, 1985

>Many SNCC people attended the reception. I am coming to know Ethelbert Miller who I look forward to coming to know well. He told me, "I'm going to look after you." I don't know why he thinks I need looking after. Arlo and Jorma were there and they helped tremendously by greeting people at the door. It was all in the garden of the Stewart Mott House – a most beautiful summer evening – held together by Cordell Creedle's music. Beautiful Cordell."

The New York reception was held on October 4th at the Viacom Center on West 43rd Street. Open Hand's publicist, Lucy Ann Kerry, made most of the arrangements. We sent out invitations to everyone on the SNCC mailing list. The invitation said, "It is Open Hand's sincere desire that this book serve not only as a reminder of where we were, but also as a guide to concerned people everywhere." William Kunstler and Professor John Hope Franklin were guest speakers. SNCC Freedom Singers, Matt Jones and Cordell Reagon sang. It was also Jim's fifty-seventh birthday, and there was a huge birthday cake. Many of those who attended had not seen one another since the 60s.

When we were planning for the event, Jim insisted that I invite my sister, her two daughters, and their husbands.

I was very much opposed to the idea, but Jim, as usual, was very persuasive. When I said, "We can't do that. One of my sister's son-in-laws works for the CIA," Jim replied, "All the better. It's guaranteed that the CIA will be there. Now we'll know who it is." They came, and it was not a problem. I think they enjoyed the occasion. My sister told me later how much she liked hearing Professor Franklin.

◊ ◊ ◊

Bess loved the book **The Little Bitty Snake** and she went out of her way to help promote it. Unbeknownst to me, she had business cards printed with her name and the title New York Sales Representative Open Hand Publishing Inc. Equipped with her newly printed business cards and copies of all three language versions of **The Little Bitty Snake**, Bess made a call on the buyer of the New York Public Library's gift store. They immediately placed an order for multiple copies of each version of the book, and they continued to reorder for years to come.

◊ ◊ ◊

The week following the reception for **The Making of Black Revolutionaries** I participated in the New York Book Fair held in Madison Square Garden, which featured small and independent presses. They were beginning to be recognized as an essential sector of the publishing industry. Setting up my table, I felt very small and insignificant in the huge cavernous space. Looking around the room, I became conscious that it was filled with white people. Later, while walking around, I came across the combined display of *Africa World Press* and *Red Sea Press*. I became engaged in a conversation with the publisher and assistant publisher, Kassahun Checole and Pamela Sims. They were both very warm and friendly, and we decided we could promote one another's titles by my including some of their titles on my table and their including Open Hand titles on their table. Later, we decided it would benefit each of us if we were to include some of one another's titles in each of our catalogs. For many years to come some titles from *Africa World Press* appeared in the Open Hand catalog and some Open Hand titles appeared in the *Red Sea Press* catalog.

Open Hand's first catalog came out in 1986. Designed by Gail Peck, it included a mission statement:

> OPEN HAND *is a symbol for sharing and cooperation.* OPEN HAND PUBLISHING INC. *was created with the objective of making available books to nurture the spirit as well as inform. Because we are not afraid to go against the current of popular thought, we are able to make available important books which otherwise might remain unpublished. Hopefully, this will help to bring about an era of greater understanding and harmony among people.*

◊　◊　◊

My sister's support of Open Hand surprised me. I come from a conservative Republican family and, for the most part, we avoided discussion of political issues with each other. Bess disapproved of my relationship with Jim and would not invite him to her apartment. And yet, she continued to accept and love me. She did not disown me as I expect my parents would have done had they known of my involvement with a black man. They were good people, but they were a part of a society that was strictly segregated. There was almost no opportunity in their world for people of different races to become acquainted.

49

As a child my actual contact with people of color was limited to talking with our black gardener, Fred Dial. As a teenager I had felt overprotected and isolated from most of the world, as indeed I was. After I turned 16 and got my driver's license, Mother sometimes asked me to drive Fred a couple of miles to where he could catch a bus home. Once, as I was driving him to the bus stop, he told me his daughter was studying at the University of Buffalo to become a social worker. Prior to this, when I was in tenth grade, I had decided that I wanted to become a social worker. So, one day when Fred's daughter came to our back yard looking for her father, I was eager to talk with her. I wanted to invite her into the house and ask her about the university and about her classes. And then I realized, I could not ask her into the house...that she was black...that no black person had ever been invited into our house...that my parents would disapprove...that if I asked her in, they might ask her to leave...and that would be terrible. So I let the opportunity pass, and in doing so I realized that this was not my home, but my parents' home.

◊ ◊ ◊

I knew so little about those years in the South when Jim was in constant threat of assassination. As the leader of SNCC, he was responsible for making life and death decisions that would impact many people. More than a decade had passed, but in many ways he was like a soldier home from battle; constantly on guard and seldom able to relax, even in the privacy of home. For me, it was too much. I wanted to be able to laugh, have friends over, and engage with the world in ways that were other than political. Neither of us was able to face up to the fact that our differences were irreconcilable and we should each go our own separate way. Instead we developed a sustained partnership that revolved around working for social change.

I continued to see Jim as that sweet young man with the sparkling eyes that I had known before there was a civil rights movement. I think it was important for him to have someone there who saw him from that perspective.

In spite of the strain in our personal relationship, we always continued to work closely together. I don't recall now what the incident was, but something tragic had happened that prompted me to ask him, "Don't you ever cry?" to which he replied, "I have no tears left."

◊ ◊ ◊

Open Hand's publicist, Lucyann Kerry met William Loren Katz, an author who was looking for a publisher for a book he had written about the impact of the Ku Klux Klan on American history. Lucyann thought his book would be a good match for Open Hand. She set up a meeting at his apartment on West 13th Street in the Village, which also served as his office. It was an easy walk from my sister's apartment next to Grace Episcopal Church on 10th and Broadway. Katz, a man in his mid-forties, like myself, was personable and easy to talk with. I was impressed when I learned that he had spent a lifetime researching black history, and had compiled a vast collection of historic photographs of African Americans. He was the author of more than a dozen books that had been published by major publishing companies, but he could not find a publishing company that would publish his book about the Ku Klux Klan.

I never had any personal experience with the Klan, and I thought of it as only having existed in the South. But, as Bill Katz talked, I began to realize that the Ku Klux Klan was still a powerful organization that should be taken seriously. I was shocked to see photographs from the 1920s of the streets in Washington, DC filled with people marching in white Klan robes and hoods. Thinking that Open Hand could play a role in educating people about the Klan, I decided to publish **The Invisible Empire: the Ku Klux Klan Impact on History**. The book examines the political impact of the Ku Klux Klan on US life and policies. It is illustrated with rare photographs and vintage drawings from Katz's vast collection. I wrote promotional material for the book: "In its early years, the Klan focused on terrorizing ex-slaves and their white supporters. In the 1920s, it directed its attention to union members, Catholics, and Jews. More recently, it has regrouped as an armed, heavily financed covert effort to 'recapture' the US government 'for white people.'"

Now, in 2020, a shiver goes down my spine as I reread this last sentence, written when the book was published, 34 years ago in 1986. Today Donald Trump, sitting in the White House, speaks favorably about white nationalists and selects them to be his advisors. I never thought it would come to this.

While we were negotiating about **The Invisible Empire** Bill Katz told me his most well-known book, **The Black West** published by Doubleday in 1971, was out of print. When I expressed an interest in bringing out a new edition, Katz was very responsive to the idea. No commitment was made at that time.

To date, Open Hand had no formal contracts with its authors, just a letter of agreement, so drawing up a contract was a challenge and I did not know where to begin. This had never been discussed in the *Publishing Specialist Program* at GWU. With a little research, I discovered several boilerplate contracts, and selected one. Shortly after Bill Katz signed it, Open Hand's designer, Gail Peck began working on the layout for **The Invisible Empire**.

◊ ◊ ◊

I also signed a contract with E. Ethelbert Miller for his second book of poetry, **where are the love poems for dictators?** Ariel Dorfman said of this book, "These poems are full of savage, nostalgic tenderness –a fit answer to a world where violence threatens to drive us all mad and the media has robbed language of its meaning." If I recall correctly, with the help of a typesetter, I designed this book. It featured very strong illustrations by a Washington, DC artist, Carlos Arrien. Open Hand was emerging as a viable publishing company.

◊　◊　◊

The house Danny and Gail Peck and I rented was to be sold and we had first option to purchase it. We loved the house and hated the thought of moving. We briefly considered buying it together, but reason prevailed. Much as I enjoyed Danny and Gail's company, I didn't want to marry them. Once again, I searched for a place to live and soon found a pleasant three-room apartment on the second floor of an old house that had been divided into three apartments, one on each floor. It had bay windows overlooking Seward Square, just a three-minute walk from the Open Hand office at Eastern Market. I hung a hammock on the small back porch overlooking a vast uncared for green area resembling a jungle in the middle of Capitol Hill. My cat, Chestnut, happy to no longer have to share territory with the Peck's animals, enjoyed climbing down a tree that grew just inches from the porch.

August 31, 1985

> *I have found a "nest". A tiny apartment on Capitol Hill just near Open Hand, that seems quite ideal. It is very light and surrounded by trees with a*

wooden porch on the back. I just happened to spot a sign "For Rent" in the window, and I feel as though it was made for me.

◊ ◊ ◊

Linda Sanders left Open Hand after finding a full time job and I was without an assistant. Vicki Johnson suggested I interview Samuel who had recently immigrated to the US. Mehret was living with her sister, a close friend of Vicki's. Mehret was Eritrean, had grown up in Ethiopia, and then graduated from college in the US. Most recently, she had been living in Kenya with her husband and three children. Circumstances were such that she was forced to flee to the US, leaving her family behind. I felt a close bond with Mehret, who, like me, had young children living far away. Working with her was always a pleasure and I learned a great deal about people and life in northern Africa. She remained with Open Hand for about a year before getting a full-time job as a librarian.

Open Hand's office above the flower shop was so comfortable and convenient. My landlord, who was the owner of the flower shop below, brought me flowers and I felt as though we were on the best of terms. I could scarcely believe it when one day he sent a messenger to tell me that I would have to move within 30 days. He gave no reason. Once again, I went searching for office space, and I found it in a building on the corner of Pennsylvania Avenue and 19th Street, across from George Washington University. In good weather I bicycled to work through the Mall, passing through the Ellipse, the park just south of the White House. It was not unusual to see Ronald Reagan's helicopter taking off or landing. On winter days when it was too cold to ride a bicycle, or in summer when it was too hot, I rode the Metro.

◊ ◊ ◊

So much in publishing depends upon whom you know. In addition to being interesting and informative, monthly meetings of the *Washington Publishers' Association* provided an excellent opportunity to meet the right people. I looked forward to the November 1985 meeting when the topic was *Writing, Illustrating and Publishing Children's Books.* While waiting for the program to begin, I became engaged in conversation with the African-American woman seated next to me. When I mentioned that I was publishing books about African-American history and that I was looking for someone who could teach me how to do accounting on a computer, the woman replied, "My nephew does that sort of work. I will ask him to give you a call."

Within a few days I received a telephone call from Phillip Morris explaining that his aunt had asked him to contact me. We made an appointment to meet at my office. Phillip Morris, who I learned was an accountant at the Naval Institute Press, took me under his wing. My small computer was adequate for him to set up an accounting system using DacEasy software. He taught me how to input data. At the end of each month Phillip would arrive at my office to do the necessary end-of-month routine. This was all done on a volunteer basis as he would accept no payment. I remain ever grateful to Phillip Morris for the many hours he spent steering me through the mysteries of accounting and computing.

◊ ◊ ◊

1986 was the first year that Open Hand had a catalog. Featured in it were **Self- Determination, The Making of Black Revolutionaries, Sammy Young, Jr., The Little Bitty Snake**, and **The Invisible Empire.** In addition, there were four titles of books published by Africa World Press: **The**

Roots of Crisis in Southern Africa, **Agribusiness in Africa**, **Nambika: Studies of Women in African Literature**, and **Hell-Hole Robben Island**. It was most unusual to have a children's book amidst this heavy political subject matter, but from the beginning it was my intention to develop a line of children's books that would empower young people and promote social justice.

◊ ◊ ◊

After Mehret's departure, Katherine Flaherty, whom I met at a *Women of Wealth* meeting, became my assistant. Kathy had been a Peace Corps volunteer in Central America and was involved with the *Sojourners*, helping to bring political refugees across the Mexican border. We enjoyed working together. At lunchtime we often joined a protest in front of the White House, only about a ten-minute walk up Pennsylvania Avenue.

◊ ◊ ◊

I worked hard arranging the publicity for a fundraising party for the Unemployment & Poverty Action Council (UPAC) at which James Baldwin was the guest of honor. It was held at the Mott House. Baldwin captivated us all with an account of trying to cash a check in Florida in the 1960s. His friend said to him "You can't cash a check in Florida." Nevertheless, Baldwin decided to try. It was mid-afternoon and the bank manager announced, "The bank is closed." Baldwin went back at 9 am the next morning and was again told, "The bank is closed." James Baldwin had us all laughing over this tragic example of segregation.

Some months later James Baldwin came to Washington again to give a lecture at the Library of Congress. That evening I wrote in my journal:

April 28, 1986

> There was one point in particular that struck home. I recall my longing those early years in Australia to see black people. The composition of the Australian population seemed so bland. What Baldwin said tonight made that longing more comprehensible. He said that white people in the United States are different because they are the only white people who have experienced black people. In Europe the white people are still in a state of innocence. White people in the United States try to deny their black experience and pretend they are still in that state of innocence. But one who goes on pretending to be innocent becomes grotesque.
>
> And this is part of why I needed to return to the United States. I needed to develop more fully an understanding of a total society and not just a white society, and on the basis of that understanding, to participate in helping to build a better world.

◊ ◊ ◊

One evening shortly after moving into the apartment on Seward Square I phoned the children in Seattle. Jorma was 13 at the time. As soon as I heard his voice I knew that something was wrong. He told me that he and three of his friends had come out of a movie in downtown Seattle after midnight and they had been attacked. "I was beaten up. Don't tell Dad." Up until then, I thought all was well with the children. Suddenly, I knew I had been mistaken. The question arose in my mind as to whether I needed to return to Seattle to live. I began thinking seriously about the steps that I would need to take in order to move across the country and still preserve Open Hand.

By June, when Arlo and Jorma arrived for the summer, I had decided that come January I would return to Seattle to live. It would take several months to close down the Open Hand office and to make arrangements to open a new office in Seattle.

Arlo attended a summer workshop on filmmaking at the Smithsonian, and Jorma attended soccer camp. It was always hard at the end of the summer when the children returned to Seattle. This year I looked forward to moving back to Seattle in December.

August 19, 1986

> *I have spent the evening putting memories away. The children left yesterday. Tonight I'm picking things up around the house – a ball on which Jorma had drawn a face, our camping gear, Arlo's drawing books – little things, little memories.*

◊ ◊ ◊

The Reagan administration supported the Contras who were fighting to overthrow Nicaragua's elected socialist government, the Sandinistas. There was strong support in the US for the Sandinistas and, over the past few years, thousands had come to march on the Mall to protest Ronald Reagan's Central American policy. Demonstrations and actions were taking place all around the country.

On November 1, 1986, four Vietnam and WWII veterans began the *Veterans Fast for Life* on the steps of the Capitol building. Peace activists came from all over the world to stand in solidarity with the veterans. Several senators and congressmen came out and expressed their support. Each afternoon at 4 o'clock, I joined dozens of other people who gathered on the Capitol steps to support the veterans. One of those afternoons I found myself standing next to a peace activist who had just flown in from Germany. I was astounded when, one of the first things she said to me was, "I am looking for a publisher for my book about German women in WWII." I replied, "I'm a publisher, but I publish books about African-American issues."

The purpose of the fast was to raise awareness among the American public and to escalate opposition to Reagan's policies. But the *Washington Post* and the *New York Times* printed nothing about the fast, even after it had gone on for over a month. They would not even print the Letters to the Editor that were sent in about it. Finally, on October 15, the veterans were invited to appear on the *Phil Donahue Show*. The fast ended two days later when they decided they had accomplished the goal of alerting the public.

I kept in touch with the German peace activist I had met on the Capitol steps. Her name was Lilo Klug.

◊ ◊ ◊

In November, Open Hand released its fifth title, **The Invisible Empire: The Ku Klux Klan Impact on History.** I made arrangements for the author, William Loren Katz to come to DC for a media blitz that included the *Fred Fisk Show* and *America's Black Forum*. Obtaining the interviews became easier as Open Hand gained recognition. Bill Katz told me how much he was enjoying the trip to DC. He announced he was going to remain an extra two days. This was at my expense. I thought it strange, but I said nothing and paid the bill.

◊ ◊ ◊

November 6, 1986

Tuesday was Election Day and the Democrats won back the Senate with an overwhelming majority. This will bring about the end of Reagonism as we have known it and usher in a new era that I find most positive and hopeful. Our lowest point was when Congress approved aid to the Contras in Nicaragua, about 2 months ago – but many positive things have been happening, best of all the placement of sanctions on South Africa.....

And now, just at this high point, I am returning to Seattle. I feel strange about this – and as though I am venturing once again into the unknown because I don't see how I will be able to maintain my political involvement from there.

Yesterday was a high point also because Jim and I went out to George Mason University where he gave a talk to the Progressive Student Association. It was raining so hard, and I took a few wrong turns along the way. Nevertheless, we arrived on time. Jim's talk was excellent and there was a good response from the students. He wants to do more lecturing on campuses. It has been so difficult to get to this point – I hate to leave. Perhaps before I leave I can organize for someone else to schedule lecturing engagements for Jim. It has taken 5 years to build up this momentum – it can't be allowed to be lost. Yesterday Jim said nothing about security, and worrying about it no longer seems to be an obstacle.

◊   ◊   ◊

On December 11, 1986, there was a book party, held in the Longworth House Office Building, in celebration of the publication of **where are the love poems for dictators?** The author, E. Ethelbert Miller arranged the event. I was fortunate indeed to have an author who had the capability to hold such a festive party in such grand surroundings. Ethelbert's parents came down from New York. Many of my friends, including Jim, were there. I had to do nothing other than stand up and say a few words. To stand and speak from a podium in the Longworth Building was challenge enough, and I was very thankful for the training in public speaking I had received the previous year.

◊ ◊ ◊

Shortly before Christmas, I watched as movers packed everything from the Open Hand office, and from my apartment, into a moving van. The driver said it would take him about three weeks to make the trip across the country. In the meantime, my plan was to drive my new Ford Aerostar van to Salt Lake City, via Kansas, en route to Seattle. With me were two precious belongings; my faithful companion, Chestnut, and my computer, which I packed as gently as if it were made of eggshells. Arlo and Jorma flew to Lawrence, Kansas where I met them at the airport. Arlo, on a learners permit, drove us all the way to Seattle via Salt Lake City where we celebrated Christmas with my dear friend, Gail Della Piana, who I had visited en route to Washington five years earlier.

3.

Seattle

1987 - 2001

Arlo, Jorma and I were so exhausted after arriving back in Seattle at midnight on January 1 that we didn't unpack the car until the next morning. I was most anxious to see how the computer had weathered the cross-country trip. After setting it up on a table and plugging it in, I held my breath. Miraculously, the screen lit up and it looked just as it had before I last turned it off in DC.

My house had an aboveground finished basement with its own entrance that worked well as Open Hand's office. I unpacked the brass plate from the office on Pennsylvania Avenue that said OPEN HAND PUBLISHING INC. and screwed it onto the outside door. There was plenty of room in the new office for three large desks, filing cabinets, and the copy machine. I built storage shelves and Arlo built a large table to be used for packing books. The commute from home to work could not have been more convenient -just down the stairs.

At the time of my arrival back in Seattle, Open Hand had six published books and three in development. There was a lot of work to be done and I was very eager to get going in the new location. Prior to moving, I had contacted a private mailing service and established Open Hand's new

Seattle address. It was on the 1987 catalog, which Gail Peck had designed when I was still in DC.

600 East Pine, Suite 565
Seattle, WA 98122

Orders began arriving and no time was lost in continuing business in the new location. My workday began at 7 am each day when I went to the office to make phone calls to the East coast. Night rates applied until 8 am, so by making calls early in the morning phone expenses were reduced. After a break for breakfast, each day began with a trip to the postal service, about a mile away, to pick up the mail. Email and fax were still unheard of, so all orders, manuscripts, and correspondence arrived in the mail.

The first few months back in Seattle I was exceedingly busy visiting bookstores and reestablishing old contacts. I found an accountant named Larry Richter. It was a relief that he was familiar with DacEasy, the accounting system that Phillip Morris had set up. At the end of each month, for the next 10 years, I sent Larry data, and he maintained Open Hand's accounts and prepared tax forms. They were in good hands. I was thankful to have found someone so trustworthy and competent.

◊　◊　◊

February 22, 1987

I regret not having written more in this journal during the period of transition. But, I've just been so busy – mornings I generally jump out of bed by 7 and rush down to the Open Hand office, now, in the basement. From 7 to 8 I make phone calls to the East Coast so as to be on night rates. Lately, I've developed the habit of writing until about 10:30 AM, then taking a break for breakfast. This is on the weeks when Arlo and Jorma are not here. When they are here, we get up about six, have breakfast together, then they are off to catch the bus to school by about 7. It is wonderful being with Arlo and Jorma. They are both bright and happy. Yesterday Arlo passed his driver's test, so he now has a license

Open Hand is moving quickly – so quickly that I'm having a difficult time keeping up with it. Need to find someone to work with me very soon. I need an office manager so as to free me to do more PR work with buyers and the media.

◊ ◊ ◊

My hands were full with all the work that needed to be done and needing to find an assistant. One evening, when I went with my friend, Joyce Zerwekh, to see a movie, she introduced me to Karl Zanzig and his wife, Amy. They had recently moved to Seattle from Missoula, Montana, and Karl was looking for a job. He had been a peace activist who had spent 6 months in jail for having entered and shut down a nuclear missile silo. The silo was located on land belonging to a farmer, sympathetic to the peace movement, who gave permission for protests to be staged on his property. Karl had no office or computer experience. I asked him if he would like to work for Open Hand and he decided to give it a try. He worked Mondays, Wednesdays and Fridays from 9 am to 2 pm packing and shipping books, and maintaining sales records. I taught him how to use the DacEasy accounting program. Karl quickly mastered every task. He was good company and we enjoyed working together.

I paid assistants an above minimum wage salary, and regretted that Open Hand was not financially secure enough to pay for health insurance. I did not have any myself and I was not receiving any income from Open Hand. Most of the orders we received were for the Forman books. **The Little Bitty Snake** was also selling reasonably well. Sales of **where are the love poems for dictators?** jumped after Ethelbert had a reading at the Library of Congress. I regretted not being able to attend.

The book about the Ku Klux Klan was still in production. I became alarmed after reading in the local press about how active the Klan, also known as the Aryan Nation, was in the Northwest. It had a strong contingency based in Coeur d'Alene, Idaho. They owned property and had a heavily armed encampment on Whidbey Island, only about an hour's drive north of Seattle. This gave me concern about my own safety and, more importantly, the safety of my children.

◊ ◊ ◊

Each Tuesday afternoon, I took time from work to meet Arlo and Jorma in front of Roosevelt High School. Then we drove up to Snoqualmie Pass and went skiing. The slopes were illuminated after dark so we had about 3 hours of skiing before heading home.

◊ ◊ ◊

I soon became very active in Seattle Women Act for Peace (SWAP), the Seattle branch of Women Strike for Peace. My involvement in the peace movement paralleled my publishing life. Shortly after returning to Seattle I attended a SWAP meeting where I met Carol Hoyt, who had moved to Seattle from Buffalo. It turned out that Carol's ex-husband and I had been high school classmates at the Park School of Buffalo. Carol and I became fast friends. She was

66

up-to-date on many of my old friends who I had lost track of during the 17 years I lived in Australia. Carol gave my forgotten childhood back to me.

◊ ◊ ◊

In March, I flew to London where Open Hand had a table at the *Radical Black Book Fair*. The books were well received and I signed a contract with a British distributor, *Central Books*. For years to come we received small but consistent orders from them, and payment was always on time.

◊ ◊ ◊

My mother-in-law, Gladys Rodieck, lived only a few miles away. While visiting her one afternoon I met Pat Andrus who was doing light housecleaning for Gladys. As Pat and I talked, we each recalled having met earlier when our children attended Stevens Elementary School. Pat and I had many common interests and we became close friends. She is a poet and we often discussed literature.

◊ ◊ ◊

The American Booksellers Association held its annual meeting in Washington, DC. Jim Forman, Bill Katz, and Ethelbert Miller all came and signed books. It was wonderful being back in DC and seeing many friends.

Bill Katz asked if I would be interested in publishing a book by a friend of his, James Yates, born in Quitman, Mississippi in 1906, the son of sharecroppers. At 16 he escaped Mississippi by hopping a freight train to Chicago. There, after graduating from Englewood High School, he found work as a dishwasher, stockyard worker, and dining car waiter. He helped organize the *Dining Car Workers Union*, a major step in Black trade union history. In 1935 Yates raised money for medical supplies for Ethiopia when it was being invaded by Mussolini's troops. In 1937 he joined the volunteers from many countries in the fight to defend the democratically elected government of Spain against Franco's fascist forces. Yates was one of the 2,800 American volunteers making up the Abraham Lincoln Brigade. Of them, there were about 100 African Americans. The United States military was still segregated at that time.

James Yates had self-published his memoir **Mississippi to Madrid: Memoir of a Black American in the Abraham Lincoln Brigade**. It was poorly edited and difficult to understand. I decided to edit and republish it.

◊ ◊ ◊

Bill Katz book **The Black West** was the first book Open Hand published after moving to Seattle. I greatly missed having Gail Peck nearby to do the design work. I found a design company in downtown Seattle to design the cover, and obtained permission from Doubleday to use the formatting of the original edition of the book. Bill Katz wrote a new chapter, "Black Women of the Last Frontier," that was not in the original book. Using the skills I had learned in the *Publishing Specialist Program* at George Washington University, I worked on my living room floor laying out and pasting the photos and type onto cardboard to be sent to the printer. There were many technical problems with both the typesetter and the printer, but by the end of the year **The Black West** was available in both cloth cover and paperback editions.

◊ ◊ ◊

Rainier Valley, on Seattle's south side, is the most ethnically diverse part of the city. When I decided to participate in an outdoor literary event at the Rainier Branch Library, I had no idea how beautiful it would be, situated on a grass-covered, tree-lined hillside adjacent to the library. Everyone was in a festive mood on the warm late-summer day. With Open Hand's books displayed in front of me, I sat at a small table watching the people. Some looked at the books and asked questions. A small energetic woman with long curly dark hair picked up **where are the love poems for dictators?** Turning to me she said, "E. Ethelbert Miller. I know him. I didn't know about this book." Thus began a long friendship with Selma Waldman, an extraordinary artist and political activist. Later, Selma invited me to her house to see dozens of books she had illustrated for the *African National Congress* (ANC). I don't think she knew Ethelbert personally, but she knew his poetry.

◊　◊　◊

Arlo graduated from high school and was preparing for a return trip to Australia that would last an indefinite amount of time.

◊　◊　◊

In July 1987 I flew to Managua, Nicaragua to attend *Festival Internacional del Libro, Nicaragua*. This trip was the adventure of my lifetime. Nicaragua, a small country with a brilliant spirit, is located between Honduras and Costa Rica. In 1979 the democratic socialist Sandinista National Liberation Front (FSLM) overthrew the brutal Samosa dynasty that had ruled Nicaragua for four decades. The new revolutionary government, with its policies promoting literacy and health care for all, was widely acclaimed by people around the world. However, the United States was opposed to the leftist Sandinista Government, and in

1981 established an economic blockade against Nicaragua. The Nixon Administration threatened military intervention and secretly funneled money to the Contras who were attempting to overthrow the democratically elected Sandinista Government. The Book Festival was held in the midst of a civil war.

Ernesto Cardinal, Jesuit priest and renowned poet, was Nicaragua's Minister of Culture. While attending the Frankfurt Book Fair in 1985 he talked about Nicaragua's lack of books with his longtime friend Peter Weidhaas, who was director of the Fair. In 1984 a major earthquake had completely destroyed Nicaragua's National Library and most of the books in the whole country were destroyed. Peter Weidhaas suggested that if Nicaragua were to hold an international book festival, publishers from around the world would come with books to leave there. That is exactly what happened. More that four hundred publishers from over 43 countries came to Managua. The minute I learned of this Book Festival, I knew I had to be there.

Because of the economic embargo the United States placed against Nicaragua it was not possible to fly there directly. I flew to Mexico City, and then on to Managua on Air Nicaragua. Taking off from Mexico City, I could only pray that the very old, tattered airplane would last out the journey.

Publishers from the United States knew in advance we would all have to share one small booth. What we didn't know was that the United States Information Service would occupy half of that booth. A great struggle for display space broke out when some of the more aggressive independent publishers began demanding space that had been allotted to the Information Service. The arguing did not stop, even when the Nicaraguan organizers of the Book Festival explained to the upset publishers that for the sake of diplomacy Nicaragua needed to keep peace with the United States Information Service and the Embassy. Besides, Nicaragua desperately needed the literature on agriculture that they would donate. The dispute was finally resolved when a large room divider, borrowed from the Cuban booth, no less, was brought over and erected. It created a physical divide between the two US contingencies.

The week-long Book Festival consisted of literary events, discussions, recitals, concerts, sightseeing, feasting and festivities. It culminated in a symposium led by President Daniel Ortega, flanked by his entire cabinet. After giving a welcoming speech, the President opened the floor to questions on any subject from anyone in the audience. The openness of the government was remarkable. In conclusion, one publisher from each geographic region was invited to present books, representative of their part of the world, to Daniel Ortega. I was astounded, and terrified, when I was invited to be the presenter for North America. Along with several books from other publishers, I handed Daniel Ortega a copy of Open Hand's bilingual children's book **The Little Bitty Snake/ La Vibora Chiquilina**. After holding it up to the audience, he gave me a warm hug and kissed my cheek.

July 25, 1987 Managua

> *Radiant expressions on people's faces despite terrible poverty. No housing, terrible transportation, poor clothing. But the people understand that now they are the owners of their own destiny. The miracle of happiness can be attributed to the revolution.*
>
> *Nicaraguans today have had to suffer to create happiness for future generations. This mood is called "The tenderness of the people."*

◊ ◊ ◊

Each year Seattle celebrates Labor Day weekend with a huge 4-day music festival called Bumbershoot. For many years, the festival included a book fair where publishers from the Northwest displayed their books and authors read from their work. It was a festive gathering of the literary community. Arlo and Jorma helped me out in minding the Open Hand booth. All three of us worked together selling books and answering people's questions.

The Bumbershoot Festival gave me a rare opportunity to meet and talk with other local publishers. I met Tree Swenson of Copper Canyon Press, who invited me to visit her in Port Townsend. Some months later, I made a trip out there and Tree showed me all about the office. They did their own shipping and had an elaborate system for packaging books. She wanted to invite me to her home for dinner, but her partner, Sam Hammil was not up to company.

I had little contact with the folks at Seal Press, a feminist press and the most established independent press in Seattle. But, once, after I moved back to Seattle from DC, the publisher and the accountant invited me out to lunch. They had not yet converted to doing accounting on a computer and they wanted to know what my experience with that had been. I always felt some friction with the various feminist presses – I felt that they thought my publishing books written by men was letting the feminist cause down.

Red and Black Books, a thriving feminist bookstore in Seattle, was located not far from where I lived. The buyer, Red Reddick, was always exceedingly supportive of all of Open Hand titles. Extremely knowledgeable about the literary world, Red would sometimes make a suggestion about an area or topic that would be suitable for a new book from Open Hand.

I was once shocked when a buyer in a feminist bookstore back East told me, "We are not interested in stocking **The Little Bitty Snake** because it was written by a male."

This felt like a personal insult as each book I published was like a child to me. I had to be in love with a manuscript before deciding to publish it. Much time, energy and money was spent on each book. It was emotionally painful to have one rejected by a bookstore buyer.

◇ ◇ ◇

In September, I received a response from Lynn Holst of *American Playhouse* to my request to have **Sammy Younge Jr.** made into a play for *Public Television* (PBS). She phoned to tell me they were most interested. If that were to happen it would change the lives of everyone involved with Open Hand. I eagerly awaited another phone call. It wasn't until almost Thanksgiving that a call came from a lawyer representing *American Playhouse*. They wanted to purchase an 18-month option for $17,500, with no up-front payment. If, after 18 months, they decided not to produce it, Open Hand would receive nothing. This was not exactly what I was hoping for, but after discussions with Jim, and with Lucyann Kerry, we decided to accept the offer. On December 9, I flew to New York to meet with the *American Playhouse* staff and sign the option. Jim and Lucyann were at the meeting. It was agreed that PBS would pay Lucyann for writing the script.

◇ ◇ ◇

Tuesday December 1, 1987

It was on the phone this morning, while talking with Lucyann, that she told me James Baldwin had died. Ethelbert told me that Gwendolyn Brooks described James Baldwin as "love personified."... Frail and strong, serious and funny, embraced by the love of millions yet alone, caring for others and needing to be cared for, brilliant yet humble – It feels like there is a great emptiness now with Baldwin gone. I feel so privileged to have met and talked with him. I smile at the memory of him at the reception in New York. It was at the end of the party and we were trying to make arrangements to see that he got home safely, when he said, "Don't worry. I can find my way. I'm a grown man," and somehow it sounded like a child speaking. Matthew Jordan drove James Baldwin home that evening."

◊ ◊ ◊

Following our family tradition, Arlo, Jorma and I opened Christmas presents in the morning and went to a movie in the afternoon. It had been a tremendously busy year and there had been times when I was so exhausted that I did not know if I would be able to go on. It was fine being back in Seattle. Open Hand was sustaining itself financially and everything seemed to be on the right trajectory.

◊ ◊ ◊

The Black West looked beautiful when it arrived from the printer. Bill Katz stayed at our house when he came to Seattle for a week of readings and slide presentations, the first of which was at Elliott Bay Books where celebrated authors from all over the world come to speak and read. Crossing the threshold into the old Elliott Bay Book Company in Pioneer Square was like entering sacred space. The musty smell of books, bricks and timber enveloped you. Shelves were filled to overflowing with books and magazines begging to be touched. The old oak flooring creaked as you made your way dawn the aisles and deeper into the store. Being there was a feast for all of the senses. Not far from the entrance was a staircase that led to the basement where there was a cafe and a large meeting room with walls lined with old books. This bookstore represented the very heart of Seattle.

I had also arranged for Bill Katz to give a slide presentation at the Seattle Public Library. There were several radio and TV appearances, and a meeting with officials from the Seattle Public Schools. Bill had been an advisor to the Seattle Public Schools when they began bussing during the 1970s.

I organized a reception to be held in his honor at my house. Among the guests were Bob and Mildred Reed, activists who had worked for decades on local and international peace and justice issues. Bob was the head of the Seattle chapter of the *Veterans of the Abraham Lincoln Brigade*. When I told the Reeds about plans for publishing **Mississippi to Madrid: Memoir of a Black American in the Abraham Lincoln Brigade** Bob offered to help in every way he could with the promotion of the book. We made an appointment to get together the following week at the Reed's house.

Bill Katz was clearly pleased with the response to **The Black West** and to the warm reception he received in Seattle.

◊ ◊ ◊

At the end of March E. Ethelbert Miller came and stayed with us for 9 days. Drawing upon public relations skills I had learned from Vicki Johnson, I arranged several engagements for Ethelbert, just as I had done for Bill Katz. Arlo and Jorma enjoyed Ethelbert – he was so funny and engaging, especially at the dinner table. His eye for what is going on and his intellect are so keen. I felt that he observed more about me than I cared for anyone to know.

March 25, 1988

> *Ethelbert has been here for the past nine days. His visit has been refreshing for me - someone to talk with and laugh with. But Ethelbert needs looking after too. He can't cook.*
>
> *Tonight is his and Zoe's (Anglesey) reading at the Cotton Club. Perhaps, best of all, through Ethelbert's being here I have come to know many other people.... Seeing into his life has put my own into better perspective.*

Not long after Ethelbert left, my first visit to Mildred and Bob Reed's home, just north of the ship canal, was the beginning of a long friendship. They were happy to learn more about Open Hand and the plans for publishing James Yates's book. Bob was exceedingly helpful in teaching me about the history and importance of the *Abraham Lincoln Brigade*. He also recommended that I contact Phyllis Hatfield about helping to edit **Mississippi to Madrid.** Phyllis and Bob had worked together for years, and she was both a skilled editor and knowledgeable about the history of the Spanish Civil War.

I contacted Phyllis Hatfield and we worked together on editing **Mississippi to Madrid.** It usually took at least a year from the time a contract was signed until we had the finished book. The editing process is slow. It takes four or five drafts going back and forth between the editor and the author before they both feel that the book is complete and ready to go to the designer. Phyllis and I worked together all summer editing **Mississippi to Madrid.** We were still using *WordStar*, an early word processor application.

It was not surprising to learn that Phyllis was also a friend of Selma Waldman, the extraordinary artist I had met on the lawn of the Columbia City Library. Pretty much everybody who was an activist in Seattle knew one another. I told Selma about the project that Phyllis and I were working on, and said to her that I was looking for someone to design the book. Selma suggested her daughter-in-law, Deb Figen who was a print designer. Deb was able to take over where Gail Peck left off. The continuity was particularly evident in the 1988 catalog, the first one to be produced in Seattle. It featured a photo from **The Black West**. Deb worked for Open Hand on a freelance basis. Apart from my assistant, Open Hand did not have in-house staff.

Deb had not designed a book before and designers were still working with typesetters and creating mechanicals rather than designing books on a computer. It was becoming clear that typesetters were soon to be phased out of existence. Keeping up with the changing technology was always a struggle. This was more than a decade before digital transmission, so communicating was done either in person, by letter, or by phone. Deb prepared mechanicals that I shipped to the printer via UPS. About a month later I received a *blueline* back from the printer. A *blueline* is a mock-up of the book made from photographic proofs from the negatives used for the printing plates of each page and the cover. The text appeared in blue ink on slippery cream-colored paper. It was used primarily to check for accuracy and positioning before the printing plates were made.

After receiving the blueline from the printer, the publisher has about a week to search for any errors and return the proof to the printer with comments about what must be changed. We looked for printer's errors, like ink spots, smudges and scratches, and photos that were not clear. This was not a time to make changes to the text. That should have happened in the editing phase. Any editorial changes were charged to the publisher.

Mississippi to Madrid was the first of many books that Deb designed for Open Hand. For the cover, Selma

Waldman made two drawings of Jimmy Yates, one of him as a young boy, and the other of him driving a truck of Abraham Lincoln Brigade volunteers.

Publishing a book required teamwork. I enjoyed working with Deb, and over the years we came to know one another's expectations. I can't exactly say it was fun, as it was hard work, and keeping up with the changing technology was always a struggle. But, work on each book was most satisfying.

◊ ◊ ◊

In June 1988 the American Booksellers Association convention was held in Los Angeles. I had come to know a few of the other publishers and was beginning to feel more confortable at this huge annual event. I could see from Kassahun Chicloe's booth that his companies, Africa World Press and Red Sea Press, had grown a great deal since we first met at the New York Small Press Book Fair in 1985. Apart from Africa World Press, Red Sea Press, and Open Hand, there was practically no Black representation at the ABA. Attending a booth by myself all day long was hard work. I was pleased when Bookazine ordered 100 copies of **The Black West**. I returned home feeling that what Open Hand was doing was important and that we were slowly gaining recognition, and would continue to do so.

◊ ◊ ◊

In November, after we received 5,000 paperback copies of **Mississippi to Madrid** from the printer, I set about sending press releases and review copies to the media. When I made follow-up calls in December, I was delighted to learn that both Library Journal and Publishers Weekly would be reviewing the book. Everything was coming together nicely.

◊ ◊ ◊

It was exciting to see Open Hand's list grow. I was eager to continue publishing children's books along with the adult titles. LaVerne Hall came to my office to discuss publishing a children's alphabet book to be illustrated by her ten-year old daughter, Mahji. I decided to publish **"T" is for Terrific / "T" es por "Terrifico"**, our second bilingual children's book would be a companion book to **The Little Bitty Snake**, which continued to sell quite well in spite of the fact that bilingualism was regarded at that time as undesirable. It was being fought against vehemently in most schools, as it still is today in many places. The word *multicultural* was just coming into common usage.

Deb Figen designed the new children's book. I was determined to use a local printer, thinking that with all the trees in the Northwest, it did not make sense to go elsewhere for paper. After having talked with numerous local printers, I learned that their prices were not competitive with Midwest printers. I came to the conclusion that it was best to do as everyone else was doing and have our books printed in the Midwest where printing and binding are more economical, and where most of the books in the United States are printed.

◊ ◊ ◊

When I left Seattle for Washington in 1982 *Publishers Northwest* (PNW) had been a thriving organization. Publishers, and anyone interested in publishing in the Seattle area, met once a month in the basement of Elliott Bay Books. Meetings were informative and well attended. By the time I returned from DC, attendance was so low that there were few people there other than the organizers, mostly people from Seal Press.

Attendance at these meetings continued to dwindle until the Board announced they were discontinuing the organization. I couldn't help but reflect upon how much I had benefited from the *Washington Book Publishers* meetings in Washington, DC. Thinking about how helpful it would be to have an organization like that in Seattle, I asked Duse McLean, publisher of Thistle Press, and Kent Sturgess, publisher of Epicenter Press, if they would join me in continuing *Publishers Northwest*. We asked the Board members who had just brought an end to the organization if they would mind if we elect a new Board and attempt to rebuild the organization. They had no objection. Duse and I became co-chair and Kent treasurer. We told Pat Soden, director of the University of Washington Press, about the changes and asked him if he would consider being on the Board. He agreed. Each of us on the new Board wanted to see book publishing thrive in the Pacific Northwest. To this end, we organized monthly meetings that would be of interest to a broad range of people: publishers, editors, designers, and PR people, as well as authors.

Because it had become so difficult to find parking space in downtown Seattle, we decided to change the meeting place from Elliott Bay Books to a building at the Arboretum, east of downtown. The ambiance of the arboretum, with all the magnificent fir trees and plants, made going to PNW meetings a most pleasant experience. The organization quickly revived, and there were usually 30 or 40 people at each meeting. Jerry Gold of Black Heron Press was almost always there. Duse McLean, Kent Sturgess, Pat Soden, and I came together a couple of time each year at what we called steering committee meetings. This was a great treat as we met at the Seattle Yacht Club, where Duse was a member.

◊ ◊ ◊

In July of 1988 I turned fifty. Approaching the half-century mark caused me to reflect upon those things in life that I had neglected doing. The last summer in Washington, DC I took sailing lessons on the Potomac River with the objective of learning how to sail before turning 50. That first year back in Seattle, I worked intensely all year long. I also took time off to go sailing and nourished a dream of sailing back to Sydney in a small yacht. I joined a sailing class that met at the Mt. Baker Boat Ramp on Lake Washington. The instructor told us that it is best to learn on a small craft that you can handle yourself. The skills you learn there can be transferred to a large craft. We learned to deliberately tip our craft over, then right it. That training gave me the confidence to take out a time-share on a 32-foot yacht at Elliott Bay Marina in Puget Sound. I received about 10 hours of private instruction before passing a test that qualified me to captain the *Adagio*, a beautiful ship with a galley and 4 bunks. In order to qualify to become captain of the yacht I had to first pass both written and practical tests in boat handling, navigation, and operating a 2-way radio. Of all the frightening aspects to sailing, making ship-to-shore calls on the radio frightened me the most.

I met a woman who was a very experienced sailor and we sailed all through the winter regardless of the weather, dressed as if we were going skiing. I learned the skill of docking with the motor turned off. It required complete silence and being fully aware of the speed, the weight of the boat, and the wind. By the time summer came I felt confident enough of my skills to invite friends to come for a sail with me.

◊ ◊ ◊

Manuscripts arrived almost daily. The shift from typewriter to computer was taking place. Most of the manuscripts we were then receiving had been written on a typewriter, but there were some that had been written using a computer. The tool which one uses to write definitely affects the writing. To this day, I usually write in longhand then later transcribe it onto my computer. I can't seem to think without a pen in my hand. In his book **This Old Man,** Roger Angel remarks about John Updyke's writing after he shifted to computer, "...the flavor was mysteriously different, the same wine but another year."

◊ ◊ ◊

It's funny how you meet people in unlikely places. I met Rosella Stern, a grant writer, in a water exercise class. She lived only two blocks from me and we frequently went on walks together and talked about our common interest in civil rights. When I told her about my desire to make a documentary about some of the people in SNCC and their children, Rosella was interested in working on the project. We approached John Schwab, a documentary filmmaker who also lived in our neighborhood. John, Rosella and I worked for many months on a proposal for a documentary called *Generations of Freedom*, which we submitted to the National Endowment for the Humanities.

The proposal read, "GENERATIONS OF FREEDOM is a one hour television history about the courageous young people who were a part of the Civil Rights Movement during its formative years and leading up to the passage of the Civil Rights Act of 1964. Through probing first-person interviews with these people and with their children, we will examine the lasting impact that their participation in the Civil Rights Movement has had upon them and their families, as well as the long-term reverberations it continues to have on American society. This program will be targeted for PBS broadcast and for classroom use."

◊ ◊ ◊

It was always a pleasure having Karl Zanzig as my assistant. He was smart and reliable and had become a good friend. So it came as a disappointment when he told me that he and his wife had decided they would be moving back to Missoula, Montana. After Karl left I put the word out into the community via word of mouth that I was looking for an assistant. I interviewed a young woman, Tamara Madison Shaw, and liked her immediately. She was self-assured, poised, had a strong literary background, and was herself a poet and performing artist. It seemed I always had extremely good fortune in finding staff. The job was only part-time, and I could not offer the benefits that employees deserve, but the job did afford the opportunity to learn about publishing and, to some extent, to be creative.

◊ ◊ ◊

The three-day Sundiata Festival, a celebration of black culture, is held annually at the Seattle Center. It enables people to explore and experience the roots and contemporary influences on African-American culture through live performances, hands-on activities, food, and fashion. I enjoyed being there each spring attending the Open Hand booth. I felt very welcome and Open Hand's books were well received.

It was at the Sundiata Festival that I met Thurman Holmes, a Jamaican-Canadian musician who had traveled extensively and had a sharp eye for what was going on in the world. Thurman and I became good friends. Going downtown in the evening to where he was playing piano was a relief from the pressure I was living under.

◊ ◊ ◊

Arlo departed on a trip to Australia for an indeterminate amount of time. Jorma had never been apart from Arlo for more than a week and he found adjusting to Arlo's absence difficult. Receiving a letter of acceptance to Central Washington University cheered Jorma up.

◊ ◊ ◊

On January sixth 1989, PBS notified me that they were canceling the option for *Sammy Younge Jr.* I doubted that it was a coincidence that this was the day after George H. W. Bush was inaugurated president.

◊ ◊ ◊

In February, I made a trip to Lawrence, Kansas to visit Lucyann Kerry, who was then teaching film and media at the University of Kansas. I used this opportunity to visit Larry Giddings, a political prisoner in Leavenworth Correctional Institution with whom I had been corresponding since 1981 when he placed one of the first orders for **Self-Determination and the African-American People**. Larry wrote a review of the book, which helped me to understand it better. Through corresponding with him, I became interested and involved in prison issues and was invited to the Federal Prison in Monroe, Washington to talk with a group of prisoners about writing and publishing. Over the years, Open Hand received hundreds, maybe thousands, of requests from prisoners all over the country for free books. We established the *Open Hand Prison Project* and sent all of our damaged books to prisoners. The book most frequently requested was **Self-Determination and the African-American People**. Larry told me that an inmate at Leavenworth was translating **The Invisible Empire** into Chinese.

84

It was good seeing Lucyann again. She was disappointed that American Playhouse was not going to produce the story about Sammy Younge, Jr. She had another idea for a documentary about SNCC, to be called *The Movement Revisited*, which she was pursuing through the University of Kansas.

◊ ◊ ◊

March was an unbelievably busy month. Ethelbert returned to Seattle and had a radio interview and a reading at Elliott Bay Books. Arriving on the same day as Ethelbert was Lilo Klug, a peace activist and member of the Green Party and of the City Council from Heilbronn, Germany. Lilo is the woman who told me she was seeking a publisher as we stood on the steps of the Capitol Building at the time of the Veterans' Fast for Peace. After she returned to Germany we corresponded. I decided to publish the book she had edited containing the recollections of 19 German women about their war experience. At the time of the war they had been either children or very young women. Some were part of the resistance, others were drafted into the army, and some were children caught up in the maelstrom as supporters of Hitler.

Lilo came to Seattle to work with me on translating and editing her book **Surviving the Fire: Mother Courage and World War II**. The two of us, sitting at my dining room table, translated the German edition of the book into English.

Tuesday March 21, 1989

> *The house is silent although full of people. Lilo Klug is asleep in Arlo's room. Shakurra and her two little girls, Naseema and Aisha are downstairs in the extra room, and Jorma is in his bed. Ethelbert is here too,*

but I found a beautiful suite for him in a small hotel near Volunteer Park. Everyone arrived on Sunday. Ethelbert will be giving a reading on Wednesday evening. Lilo and I are working on her manuscript.

◊ ◊ ◊

Also in progress were two more children's titles. I had fallen in love with a collection of fanciful Mother Goose-like rhymes drawn from the African-American experience. It was called *Nightfeathers*, and was written by Carletta Wilson, Seattle poet, performing artist and librarian. I found a local artist, Jody Kim to illustrate the book. Jody and Carletta worked together until the drawings were a perfect match for the poems. Then, Carletta, Jody and I met with Deb Figen who designed the book and the cover. Carletta wanted it to be a small book that would fit comfortably in the hands of a child. Carletta chose Sundara Morninghouse as her *nom de plume.*

◊ ◊ ◊

As Open Hand gained more recognition, the mailbox became flooded with submissions. Although I knew it was important for a publishing company to have a niche and focus on a single subject, I found it difficult to exclude interesting manuscripts just because they did not conform strictly to Open Hand's multicultural niche. I viewed it as my duty to read and give serious consideration to each manuscript. Most could be eliminated within a few minutes. Others deserved more time, and there was the occasional one that I read all the way through. My least favorite task was sending out rejection letters. I asked my friend, Pat Andrus, to become Open Hand's manuscript editor. The job had a nice title but was very part-time.

The chance that a publishing company will accept a manuscript is exceedingly small and over the years, Pat sent out hundreds of rejection letters. While most publishing companies only accept manuscripts from literary agents, we seldom dealt with them.

Open Hand required that manuscripts be typewritten in a particular format and that they be accompanied by a submission letter and a self-addressed-stamped-envelope. One day a heavy package arrived from Quebec that met none of these requirements. I opened it and found about 500 pages hand written with dark pencil in small lettering. It was about metaphysics and philosophy and must have taken many years to write. As there was no return address, I put the manuscript aside. In about 2 weeks I received a phone call from the author who told me he was on the road, moving from Quebec to Seattle with his family so that he would be here when his book was published. I left the manuscript, with a polite rejection letter, for him at the postal service, and did not hear from him again.

◊ ◊ ◊

In May, I flew to New York where I had an appointment with the author of **Mississippi to Madrid**, James Yates, who I had not yet met in person. It was not a long walk from my sister's apartment on Broadway and West 10th Street, where I was staying, to Yates's apartment on East 25rd Street. Wanting to appear professional and yet casual, I wore a light summer suit and sandals. Shortly before reaching his building, the strap on my sandal broke, making it impossible to walk while wearing it. So, I arrived at James Yates's door, embarrassed, with one shoe on and one shoe in my hand. When I asked him if there was a shoe repair shop in the neighborhood, he took my sandal and looked at it carefully. Then he slowly went to a cabinet, pulled out a small drawer, took out a needle and thread, and calmly commenced repairing my sandal. That was so totally Jimmy. He was resourceful, along with being friendly and kind. That was the only time we spent together, although there were many occasions that we talked on the phone.

On to DC for the ABA, and for an appointment with Barbara Sirota of the National Endowment for the Humanities to discuss the grant application for the documentary *Generations of Freedom*.

At the ABA Jim, Shakurra, and my former assistant, Kathy Flaherty were all on hand to help with the Open Hand booth.

June 9, 1989

> The ABA convention was a tremendous success for Open Hand. Within ten minutes from it's opening, Literary Distributors Inc. placed an order for 500 copies of **The Black West**, the largest order we have ever had. Several progressive publishing companies coming together to display their books generated tremendous interest. We handed out at least 1,000 catalogs and there was seldom a moment when there weren't people in the booth looking at the books. I made contact with many other publishers and distributors, which I expect will be ongoing. This conference will probably prove to be a watermark. I've decided definitely to go to the Frankfurt Book Fair in the fall.

I was searching for a book distribution company that would include Open Hand books on their list. Up until this time, Open Hand sold books directly to individuals, bookstores, and libraries. Karl or I packed and shipped each book, either via the US Post Office or UPS. I put a sign in the front window to signal to the UPS driver when we needed a pickup. That was fine when there are only a few titles, but as our titles increased I needed a distributor to handle storage, packing and shipping. In addition, a distributor would include our titles in their catalog and their sales representatives would show the books to bookstore buyers all across the country. There were only about four or five book distribution companies and it was very difficult for a small publisher to gain their attention. I spoke with Marilee Talman, owner of Talman Book Distribution out of New York; then received notice from her in the fall that she was interested.

◊　◊　◊

June 2, 1989

I probably won't live long enough to ever figure Jim out ... 200 years probably wouldn't be long enough ... even though I still keep having some faith that eventually we will get things straightened out. Things can seemingly be going along very well, then suddenly and for no apparent reason, there will be a shift marked by some cruel remark or insult.

This afternoon we met at the UPAC office, walked down to the health food store on Pennsylvania Avenue where we got something to eat, then sat at a picnic table and enjoyed lunch together. Owen Latimore died yesterday. We talked about the conference in '58 where he talked and where we met. It was a pleasant calm time together.

Then, this evening we met at NW 16th and U and went for a walk as it was growing dark. A hot summer evening. There were a lot of people out and it was fun being a part of it all. We went into a little store and bought a cold drink. Jim asked for two cups and we headed back towards a little park where we could sit and enjoy the drink. The park turned out to be a little further away than we thought so Jim suggested we find another place to sit, and I agreed. I thought everything was fine when Jim said, "Some times you have to improvise. You don't have to be so rigid," to which I replied, "I don't think I am a rigid person." Jim said, "You are a very rigid person. I said, I am nowhere near as rigid as you, and being insulted is something I don't need." When Jim said, "I guess you would rather walk home alone," I handed him the drink and the food of his, which I was carrying, and continued along alone.

And thus it always is, sooner or later. And that is why I choose not to stay at his place and be the receiver of a sudden, unexpected, unpredictable insult.

October 9, 1989

I'm worried about Jim but don't see that I can help him. He has had to give up the UPAC office on Maryland Avenue, a tremendous disappointment to him. Both phones, in the office and the apartment, have been cut off for several months. I don't know what will happen to him. He doesn't want to get a teaching position and he won't organize to be invited to give guest lectures.

◊   ◊   ◊

I was back in Seattle in plenty of time for Jorma's high school graduation. In the fall he would be off to Central Washington University, and Arlo, who was back from Australia, was enrolled at Evergreen State University. With both of the children off to college, I was ready to move into the new decade by resuming my birth name, "Johnson". I would no longer be known as Anna Rodieck.

◊ ◊ ◊

A manuscript arrived from a man named Fritz Hamilton in California that Pat Andrus, Phyllis Hatfield, and I loved and found difficult to reject. **Love, Debra** explores the life of a runaway girl, Debra, who takes the family Cadillac and runs away choosing a life of addiction and prostitution in preference to remaining in an abusive situation at home. In letters to her dead mother who lost her life to alcoholism, Debra describes her odyssey through the underworld of contemporary American street life. I made the decision to publish **Love, Debra** even though the subject matter was outside Open Hand's niche of multicultural books.

◊ ◊ ◊

In October I flew to Germany to participate in the Frankfurt Book Fair, the largest book fair on earth where publishers gather each year from all over the world to buy and sell foreign rights. Black Classic Press and Open Hand shared a booth. I had hoped to be able to take copies of **Surviving the Fire**, but, unfortunately, it had not yet arrived from the printer.

October 10, 1989

> *I seem to be finding my way around Frankfurt with ease. It surprises me a little when people under-stand and respond to my questions about directions. "Wo ist .....? Wie kann ich .....?"*
> *The organization at the Frankfurt Book Fair is wonderful. The organizers are exceedingly polite, kind,*

helpful and genuinely interested in the books we are presenting. All of this is quite a contrast to the ABA where everything is more or less thrown at you and for anything you might need, like a table, you pay extra. Here everything is provided, even a locker with a key to store your things in. This evening they even brought us sandwiches.

After the book fair, I visited Lilo Klug at her home in Heilbronn.

October 15, 1989

I arrived yesterday by train from Frankfurt and was met at the train station by Lilo and her husband Herbert. In the afternoon I went with Lilo to meet with several of the women whose stories appear in **Surviving the Fire**. *Most of them speak with a thick Schwabisch accent. I spoke Hochdeutsch and we all managed to communicate. Some of the women whose stories didn't appear in the book were naturally disappointed and Lilo explained to them about the difficulty we had with the translations and why we couldn't publish all of the stories.*

Today Herbert and Lilo took me for a drive through this most beautiful countryside. It looks so perfect, but they took me to where the Pershing Missiles are installed on the Waldheide. Problems with pollution are severe. There are no fish left in the Neckar, trees in the forest are diseased, and wild mushrooms contain such high levels of radioactivity that they cannot be eaten. All of these things are so subtle it is easy for them to be overlooked.

◊ ◊ ◊

We did not know it would happen so soon, but on November 9th, less than a month after I had returned from Germany, the Berlin wall fell. On December 2nd and 3rd US President George H. W. Bush and Soviet Premier Mikhail Gorbachev met in Malta and declared an end to the Cold War.

◊   ◊   ◊

I wanted to publish a children's book about blacks in the West to correct the mistaken image that there was no black presence on the frontier. In fact, blacks settled on this continent before the arrival of the Mayflower. I was searching for a children's book author when Bob Reed recommended I talk with Ruth Pelz who, it turned out, lived not far from me. She was a curriculum consultant to several publishers, and had written three biographical books for young readers. Ruth was interested in the project. We selected nine characters from **The Black West,** four men and three women, who played an important role in shaping the American frontier. The first, Esteven, was born in Africa, came with Spanish explorers in 1527 and explored the southwest; Jean Baptiste Ponte Du Sable, founder of Chicago; Mary Fields, a legend in Montana, Jim Beckwourth, who discovered a pass through the Rocky Mountains; Biddy Mason, one of the founding citizens of Los Angeles, and others. **It** is a 56-page book written at third grade reading level – perfect for schools.

After Ruth wrote the stories I contacted my dear friend Gail Della Piana in Salt Lake City asking her if she would illustrate them. Teaching full time and going to graduate school, Gail declined, but her husband Leandro Della Piana, a freelance artist with lots of experience working with children, illustrated the new book and we called it **Black Heroes of the Wild West**. Deb Figen designed the book and the cover. Like most of Open Hand's books, turn around time was about a year from when the contract was signed to when the books arrived from the printer.

◊ ◊ ◊

In November I participated in the Guadalajara Book Fair in Mexico. I was primarily seeking a distributor for Open Hand's bilingual children's books.

November 28, 1989 Guadalajara

> *There is lots of music and people here seem to spend time talking with and enjoying one another more than we do in the US.*
>
> *Essentially, my work here is done. I sold the Spanish language rights to* **Mississippi to Madrid***. Have left* **Self-Determination** *with a Mexican publishing company for them to consider publishing in Spanish, and have contacted numerous distributors about our children's books. Those were the goals I had set to accomplish.*
>
> *It was so interesting, selling the right to* **Mississippi to Madrid***. I sold them within the first couple of hours I was at the fair, and to the first publisher with whom I spoke... a delightful man from Spain and his wife. He speaks as little English as I speak Spanish – but almost as soon as he saw Yates' book he wanted it – his father fought in the Spanish Civil War. He knew about how difficult it was for the Americans after they returned to the US.*
>
> *He called over a translator to assist with the negotiation ... my first experience at selling rights. A little crowd of people gathered around to watch. Then, after everything was finalized, Jose, the buyer, invited me and the translator and his wife to the*

little café to celebrate. I had Coca Cola. Wow! I sold the rights for $500 and 10% of the retail price on all copies sold.

◊　◊　◊

Back in Seattle, I attended a memorial service for Huey P. Newton, co-founder of the Black Panther Party, who had been assassinated. After the service Larry Gossett, a well-known community activist who I had known for many years, introduced me to Aaron Dixon, co-founder with his brother Elmer, of the Seattle Black Panther Party. Aaron moved to San Francisco and became one of Huey Newton's bodyguards leaving Elmer as head of the Seattle Panthers. I asked Aaron, "Have you considered writing about your experience?" He said, "I would like to talk with you further about this."

On December 5th both Aaron and Elmer met with me in my office and told me their story. Aaron expressed his interest in writing about it, but there were no commitments. In addition to working, Aaron was raising two young daughters and he had little spare time. I didn't talk with him again for some time although I occasionally saw him as he was taking his children to school on the bus. After a year or so, he phoned to say that he was working on the story, and did I know of a quiet place where he could write. I told him, "You are welcome to use the desk in the spare room at my house." So, for a couple of years Aaron came to my house to write at odd times during the day - all of which must have made for interesting speculation for my neighbors. He was drop dead handsome and charismatic, not someone to go unnoticed. It wasn't until 2012, long after I had retired from publishing, that Aaron Dixon's excellent book **My People Are Rising: Memoir of a Black Panther Party Captain** was published by Haymarket Books.

◊ ◊ ◊

It was thrilling when the hardback and paperback editions of **Nightfeathers** arrived from the printer. This beautiful little book was well received at the reading and book signing at Elliott Bay Books on December 17th. This was an excellent way to round out a productive year for Open Hand.

◊ ◊ ◊

Open Hand was selling books to individuals, independent bookstores, university bookstores, and libraries across the country, as well as to the new chain bookstores, Borders and Barnes and Noble. Independent bookstores and libraries usually ordered through a wholesaler like Baker and Taylor. Karl and I became very good at packing books. Now that Open Hand had too many books to store in the basement, I rented a commercial storage space in South Seattle and had books shipped there directly from the printer. About every three or four weeks Karl and I would make a trip to the storage space and fill my van with those titles we expected would sell during the coming month. All of the lifting resulted in a nagging backache that remained with me for several years. An expensive ergonomic office chair helped to ease the pain.

As the publishing company grew I began a serious search for a distributor to sell our books and handle the fulfillment. On February 9th, 1990 I signed a contract with the Talman Company, based in New York. It became Open Hand's exclusive distributor. From that time on, the majority of our books would go directly from the printer to the Talman warehouse. At last there was a way for our books to become known to the thousands of independent bookstores all across the United States. The Talman Company, owned and operated by Marilee Talman, had a pool of salesmen, "book reps," whose job it was to introduce our books to bookstore buyers. The fact that Open Hand now had a major book distributor was confirmation of the quality of our books. Talman distributed books of about 20 highly esteemed, small, independent publishing companies. Among them was Feminist Press whose publisher, Florence Howe, I had met at the Book Festival in Managua and for whom I have high regard.

Talman required that their publishers produce four or five titles each year. Open Hand had published four titles the previous year, 1989, and I expected to continue doing that. It would require a lot of work, but it seemed that Open Hand was now in a position to become very successful. The Talman Company charged us 20% on each book sold, so Open Hand's income per book went down. I anticipated that sales would go up dramatically so that over all it would be a profitable arrangement. It appeared as though success and financial stability were just around the corner.

My personal finances had dwindled and I no longer had the ability to subsidize the publishing company. Money was needed to produce **Black Heroes of the Wild West** and **Love, Debra,** so I took a risk and borrowed $30,000 using my house as collateral. I am fiscally conservative and very opposed to incurring debt so this step was not taken lightly. The bank must have believed in Open Hand was sound or they would not have made the loan.

May 30, 1990

> *What a day. Hope there won't be many like this. Went to Cascadia Revolving Fund office to pick up check for $30,000 loan to Open Hand. Signing all the papers was quite a process. They certainly know everything about me that there ever was to know. And to think that just a few years ago $30,000 was*

like nothing to me. Well, this is what I wanted – being down to "normal" amounts of money. I really am at a point now where the need to make some money is real.

◊　◊　◊

The American Booksellers' Association convention was held in Las Vegas. Open Hand had its own booth and our books were also on display at the Talman booth. Over the years more people of color were beginning to participate in this annual event and were coming to know one another. I met Charles Taylor, publisher of Praxis Publications in Madison, Wisconsin, and Rennie Mau, publisher of Media Bridge in San Francisco. Rennie had a laptop computer, the first one I had ever seen. They were establishing a new non-profit organization, the *Multicultural Publishers Exchange Inc.* (MPE). The purpose of the organization, as stated in the by-laws, was "to encourage and support the creation, publication and dissemination of authentic information from and about different ethnic and cultural communities; and to provide opportunities for those members of the book and publishing industries who are interested in promoting and advancing the creation of multicultural materials and to provide opportunities for those members to meet and interact."

Until that year attending the ABA had been quite a lonely experience. It was so heartening to finally meet up with these kindred souls.

June 5, 1990

　　It never felt better to return to Seattle than it does today after having spent five days in Las Vegas for the ABA. The convention itself was a success for Open Hand. Booksellers from all over the nation are beginning to be familiar with Open Hand and to appreciate our books. One woman told me of the tremendous impact that **The Black West** *had upon her life.*

Open Hand's books were on display with Talman; with a special display arranged by the ABA of books by black authors; and at a combined booth of Africa World Press, Red Sea, Just Us, Black Classic, Kitchen Table and Open Hand. It was at that booth that I spent most of my time.

Some weeks after returning from Las Vegas I was surprised to receive a phone call from Frances Goldin, a literary agent I had met at the ABA. She asked if I would consider a manuscript by the well-known attorney and author, Mark Lane about President Kennedy's assassination. Although it was flattering that Mark Lane would consider being published by Open Hand, I didn't accept the manuscript, partly because it would be another deviation from our multicultural theme, and partly because I was afraid of having to deal with such a high-powered lawyer. I thought that he would demand more in the way of promotion than Open Hand would be able to deliver. In retrospect, perhaps this, like the book on Move, was a lost opportunity. Mark Lane self-published **Rush to Judgment** and it became a #1 best seller.

◊   ◊   ◊

I received word from Lucyann Kerry that a well-known film producer was very interested in making a movie based on **Sammy Younge, Jr.** There were many irons in the fire and all that was needed was for one of them to come good.

◊   ◊   ◊

The children's book **Black Heroes of the Wild West** was selling well. Its success caused me to think that it should be the first in a series of books for young readers. Like **Black Heroes of the Wild West, Pathblazers** was my idea. I wanted to publish a book about unsung African-Americans who had made contributions in the areas of civil rights, education, and the arts. When I told my friend Pat Andrus that I was looking for a local author to write the book, she suggested that I contact Marilyn Fullen. I met with Marilyn and together we selected 8 people to include in the book: Septima Clark, Jester Hariston, Josephine Baker, Thurgood Marshall, Gwendolyn Brooks, James Forman, Andrew Young, and Barbara Jordan. After Marilyn wrote the stories, I took them to Selma Waldman and asked her if she would illustrate them. Selma threw herself into the project and created several powerful drawings to illustrate each biography. Selma's ability to capture the very spirit of a person was nothing short of genius. This little book is a real treasure.

◊ ◊ ◊

During the summer Fritz Hamilton, the author of **Love, Debra**, visited Seattle and stayed at our house for three or four days. I was glad to have the opportunity to come to know him, but his book was still at the printers and I didn't attempt to arrange for any book signings.

As it turned out, sadly, Open Hand did not succeed in promoting **Love, Debra** well because the book did not fit into our multicultural niche. Had the main character, Debra not been white we probably could have done better with it. The Talman Company could not, or would not promote it. I don't know why. I have always felt bad about this, as it is a worthy book.

◊ ◊ ◊

I received a proposal from Faythe Turner, a teacher of American literature at Greenfield Community College in

Amherst, Massachusetts for an anthology of *Nuyorican* writers, Puerto Ricans living on the mainland of the US, mostly in New York City. I found the idea irresistible, and later, after having read the stories and poetry of many of the writers, fell in love with the exquisite writing. I agreed to publish a book which, after a great deal of discussion, was called **Puerto Rican Writers at Home in the USA.** This anthology features seventeen of America's Puerto Rican writers, among them poet Victor Hernandez Cruz, poet Judith Ortiz Cofer, playwright Miguel Pinero, and fiction writer Piri Thomas. Their interesting accounts of life in America not only reveal what it means to be Puerto Rican, but also what it means to be American. In publishing this book I learned about the hundreds of thousands of Puerto Ricans who, in the years following World War II, moved into the ghettos of New York City, bringing with them a tradition of story telling. This literature, influenced by two languages and two cultures, blends the color and rhythms of Caribbean lyricism with gritty New York realism.

There is no way of knowing what you are getting into when you agree to publish a book. **Puerto Rican Writers at Home in the USA** was a very large undertaking that demanded a great deal of my attention for well over a year. Deb Figen worked tirelessly on the complex layout and on the cover. Endless decisions had to be made about what to include, what to exclude, getting permissions from each of the seventeen writers, what to call it, what to put on the cover, etc., etc. Nothing came easy with this book, but in the end, when I finally held a copy of it in my hands, I felt that we had done a good job and I was proud of it.

◊　◊　◊

In the summer of 1990, Lilo Klug was on a speaking tour of the United States with Jochim, a university student activist from

East Germany who had been a prime mover in demanding the removal of the Berlin wall. The wall had fallen the previous year on November 9th. Jochim said that, judging from his experience, it takes 20 % of the people to change the government. If you can get 20%, the rest will follow.

While in Seattle Lilo and Jochim stayed at my house. They did several radio interviews, and Lilo had a reading from her book, **Surviving the Fire**, at Elliott Bay Books. The turnout was excellent. Elliott Bay was always helpful in promoting Open Hand's books. It was always gratifying to see Open Hand titles in their display windows.

Lilo, Jochim, and I went for a four-day sailing trip in the *Adagio* to Port Townsend during which time we watched as dolphins and orcas swim alongside and dove under our boat. Lilo and I talked about maybe one day sailing together in the Mediterranean, but that dream never came to fruition.

◊ ◊ ◊

Each Labor Day weekend people in Seattle flock to the Seattle Center for the Bumbershoot Festival – a time for singing, dancing, and much gaiety. Attached to Bumbershoot was a literary fair at which Open Hand, along with most of the presses in the region displayed their books. Always striving for greater visibility, I jumped at this opportunity for selling books, meeting people, and exchanging ideas.

Arlo and Jorma, both home from college, helped me carry boxes of books from the van into the Seattle Center, then set up the Open Hand display table. I enjoyed sitting on a tall stool behind the Open Hand display, surrounded by books and people. Friends and strangers stopped to look at our books and to ask questions. In the afternoon I noticed a tall young woman walking directly towards me.

I remember thinking, "I am surely going to come to know this person." She resembled a potter from New Zealand, who, more than a decade earlier, had worked with me in my studio pottery in Australia. The young woman walked up to me and introduced herself as Victoria Scott - Torie.

At that time I was without an assistant as Tamara Madison-Shaw had recently had a baby and was no longer with Open Hand. Within a few days, I offered Torie the position of publisher's assistant. She accepted and began working immediately. Open Hand's office was still in the basement of my house. Earlier, that room had been used as a pottery and occasionally I still referred to it as "the pottery."

Torie was coauthoring a book with Ernest Jones, about Sylvia Stark, an African-American pioneer. Sylvia was freed from slavery at the age of twelve and traveled the Oregon Trail by covered wagon to a California gold-mining town. In 1860, fearful of being returned to slavery because of the passage of the Fugitive Slave Act and the Dread Scott Decision, Sylvia's family, along with 60 other African-Americans, left California for British Columbia. The Starks settled on Salt Spring Island where Sylvia lived to be 106. The book is called **Sylvia Stark: A Pioneer**. It is full of historical facts, maps, illustrations, and lovely archival photographs.

I decided that **Sylvia Stark**, along with another book that was in development, **Pathblazers: Eight People Who Made a Difference,** would be companion books to **Black Heroes of the Wild West**. They would all be written at fourth or fifth grade reading level, be the same size, and have a similar appearance. We would market them together as the *Contributions Series*.

Deb Figen designed each of the books in the *Contributions Series*. Later on, in 1995, we added a fourth book to the series **Women of the Wild West,** written by Ruth Pelz and containing archival photographs. It was composed of stories of eight women from various ethnic groups that played an important role in the west during the 18th and 19th centuries; Sacajawea, Juana Briones de Miranda, Biddy Mason, Mother Joseph (Esther Pariseau), Mary Bong, May Arkwright Hutton, Kate Chapman, and Sarah Winnemucca. We hoped that this book would help make up for the way in which women and people of color had largely been omitted from the history of the west. So little historical information was available, especially about Asian and Hispanic women that we had difficulty finding enough material to make up a book.

We anticipated adding more titles to the series in the future. Each book was about a person or people who had made a contribution to American history. These books proved to be popular with adult new readers. In subsequent years we responded to the many requests we were receiving from teachers for a *Curriculum Guide* for each title. We created guides consisting of 20 pages of unbound sheets that included reading comprehension questions, topics to write and/or talk about, vocabulary, and historical information. Ruth Pelz wrote the guide for **Black Heroes of the Wild West,** and **Women of the Wild West**; Victoria Scott wrote the one for **Pathblazers**; and Ernest Jones wrote the one for **Sylvia Stark**.

◊ ◊ ◊

With few exceptions African-Americans were omitted from the telling of American history. Photographs in textbooks were almost exclusively of white people. **Black Heroes of the Wild West** and later, the other books making up the *Contribution Series* were created to bring attention to people of color who played an important role in American history. I always envisioned the *Contribution Series* would be used in schools, especially in Seattle. I was receiving a great deal of positive feedback from individual teachers who bought the books and the curriculum guides for their classrooms. Thinking that the Seattle Public Schools would be interested in including them in their curriculum I made an appointment with the textbook buyer for elementary schools. I did not know that what textbooks are used in public schools throughout the country is determined in large part by the Texas State Board of Education. Because Texas is the largest textbook market in the nation, textbooks are written to their standards. (For more about this read **As Texas Goes** by New York Times columnist Gail Collins.)

When I met with the buyer for Seattle's elementary schools and showed her our books, she expressed no interest in them. I was confused when she told me she would like a trip to Jamaica and I left her office wondering if she had suggested I offer her a bribe. I'll never know.

I pretty well gave up on selling to Seattle Public Schools until I met Tony Orange, newly appointed Commissioner to the Governor Concerning African-American Affairs. His job was to bring awareness and recognition to the long-neglected African American community. He was very interested in seeing that the *Contribution Series* be included in curriculum of the Seattle Public Schools. I thought that with his endorsement and support our books would be included in the curriculum.

I met with Tony Orange several times to discuss how best to approach the schools. He took the anitiative to make an appointment with the head buyer, who, it turned out, happened to be a black woman. It was exceedingly disappointing when, after a very brief meeting, we left her office with no explanation as to why she had no interest in the books. All I can imagine is that there is a strict formula by which books are selected and it leaves no room for innovation. Open Hand was always trying to break the mold, and the bureaucratic school system was a mold that could not be broken.

Although the Seattle Public Schools were not interested in Open Hand's multicultural books there were indications that things were beginning to change. One began to see more people of color participating at the ABA and the isolation I had experienced at previous conventions disappeared. In addition to the Multicultural Publishers' Exchange several progressive presses organized with the administration of the ABA to bring our booths together in what we called *the Progressive Isle.* The isolation we had each experienced disappeared. Booksellers enjoyed hanging out in our section of the vast convention center.

Large publishing companies, having noted the success we were having, began developing their own line of multicultural books. I could not have been more shocked than when I saw Sylvia Stark featured in a large textbook being published by Time-Life. Open Hand received no credit or mention. There was even a photograph identical to the one taken by Ernie Jones and used in **Sylvia Stark: A Pioneer.** Rather than buying the rights to that photo, they had sent a photographer to reshoot it. There was little I could do to go up against this powerful corporation.

◊   ◊   ◊

Beginning with meeting the author or the arrival of a manuscript in the mail, each book evolved in its own unique way. Days usually began with a trip to the post office on my bicycle. One morning I rode home with an unusually large package in the basket of my bicycle. Once in my office, I opened it and found dozens of black and white photographs of children...all kinds of children. The box was from Charles E. Avery of North Plainfield, New Jersey. The pictures were not sorted in any way, as you would expect a manuscript to be, and there was no text, only the title

Everybody Has Feelings. I immediately fell in love with these pictures and saw the potential for them to become a children's book. I turned to Deb Figen, asking for her ideas about how we might create a book with these photographs. Deb and I selected some of the photographs and, using very few words, created a book. Deb was brilliant – with just a few words she found a way to hold the pictures together and move the story along. Working with her was always a pleasure.

Publisher's Weekly called **Everybody Has Feelings** "a beguiling photo essay." The text was in English and Spanish. *The New Jersey Star Ledger* wrote, "Avery's love for children is evident in these candid photographs. He senses the innocence of children who play together without regard for color." At the time, there were practically no books with pictures of black and brown children, just as it was almost impossible to find a doll that was not white.

We made **Everybody Has Feelings / Todos Tenemos Sentimientos** bilingual, like **The Little Bitty Snake**. This was revolutionary at the time. Working on it was such a joy. Unlike most authors, Charles Avery gave me complete liberty in creating the book. He lived in New York City and I met him only once. One fine spring day we sat and talked, for less than an hour, while sitting on the steps of the New York Public Library on Fifth Avenue and 42nd Street. He was such a gentle soul. There ought to be more people like Charles Avery on this planet. **Everybody Has Feelings** is the only Open Hand title still in print. (Rights were sold to Gryphon House.)

◊ ◊ ◊

I need to say something about the political climate at that time. George Herbert Walker Bush had been president for a year.

January 13, 1991

On Friday the House voted to support George Bush's request to go to war against Iraq, and on Saturday the Senate also voted to support Bush - if Iraq is not out of Kuwait by January 15th. The reality of war is now weighing upon everybody. People are confronting the reality that we are apt to be plunged into a war that will be very serious and bloody. Children are terrorized. There was an article in the paper this morning about a large group of eight-year-olds sobbing on their school playground.

Vigils and demonstrations are taking place all across the country and in other parts of the world. About 1,500 people met in Gasworks Park yesterday afternoon. Tomorrow night, on the eve of January 15th, people will gather at Seattle Central Community College for a march and vigil. I don't have to encourage Arlo and Jorma to participate. They want to be there. People who have never protested in their lives are phoning the White House. Everything is changed.

"Sixty Minutes" tonight talked about the acts of terrorism that will take place against the US in retaliation against our bombing Iraq.

◊ ◊ ◊

In the spring Danny and Gail Peck, with their infant daughter Danielle, came to visit. Being together again with old friends from the East coast was a special treat, made all the nicer because Arlo and Jorma were also home. We went for an overnight trip on the *Adajio*, mooring for the night off Blake Island in Puget Sound.

◊ ◊ ◊

Selma Waldman invited me to look at her new studio space in Pioneer Square, only a few blocks from where Workshop Printers used to be located. Walking into the building, one had to pass through an empty room in order to reach Selma's studio. The moment I saw the large empty room, it occurred to me it would make an ideal office space for Open Hand. I made enquiries and found that the rent was reasonable, and the landlady, a potter (no less!) was agreeable. Within a few days Open Hand had a new location. Arlo built some strong shelving to hold the books. The new office even had a display window. Torie and I enjoyed the new space. I invited Deb Figen to join us, and it worked out well – all of us working together in a spacious room with a high ceiling.

◊   ◊   ◊

Having Open Hand's books distributed by the Talman Company eased my burden. Not having to do all the storing, shipping, invoicing, and bill collecting gave me more time to focus on book development and promotion. Sales were increasing and I felt confident that Open Hand was on the right track. I think it was about this time that the company began to break even, and it seemed as though I might soon be able to give myself a salary.

◊   ◊   ◊

The author of **Nightfeathers,** Carletta Wilson, whose **nom de plume** is Sundaira Morninghouse, came to me with the idea for a book about Kwanza. It was to be called **Habari Gani? What's the News? A Kwanza Story.** It is about how a little girl, Kia, and her family experience the seven days of Kwanzaa. Without hesitation, I thought, this book would be perfect for Open Hand, and I drew up a contract. Contacting Jody Kim to ask her if she would illustrate **Habari**

Gani was easy, as she was living in my house, downstairs, where the Open Hand office used to be before we moved downtown to Pioneer Square. We planned for **Habari Gani** to be a hardback book in full color. It was a more expensive production than **Nightfeathers** or **Everybody Has Feelings** had been. Jody showed me her wonderful illustrations as they came into being, one after another. I was confident that this book would be a tremendous success. Everything was in place now for the production of the book. Deb Figen designed the book and the cover. Author, illustrator, designer and publisher – we each had previous experience and we enjoyed working together. I felt confident that publicity and distribution was in good hands with our national distributor, the Talman Company.

Habari Gani? What's the News? was well received. It won the "1993 Best Book Award" at the Bumbershoot Bookfair and the Midwest Independent Book Publishers' Association's "Best Children's Book Award for 1993.

No question, this was a busy time. Nevertheless, there was time for other activities. On hot summer afternoons, Pat Andrus and I enjoyed swimming in Lake Washington, only a ten-minute drive from my house. Few things in life compare to floating on your back on a hot day in cold lake-water and looking up at the majestic beauty of Mount Rainier. This became a summer ritual, which Pat and I planned to continue doing until we were ninety.

Pat and I also participated in Tom Truss's improvisational dance classes. There were six or seven people in the class, one of who was an 87-year-old artist and poet, Heleri Stout.

◊   ◊   ◊

Selma Waldman wrote a biting commentary about "Hammering Man" the large post-modern sculpture by Jonathan

Borofsky that had been was erected in front of the Seattle Art Museum. This essay was worthy of publication but too short to be a book. I struck upon the idea of creating a "Littlebook", a small book to be produced in limited quantities on a copy machine. It was "Print-On-Demand"; something that is very widely used and accepted by today's book world, but was unheard of at that time. By creating a separate imprint (division) called *Littlebook*, each title could have an ISBN number, a requirement if books were to be sold to libraries and bookstores. The *Littlebook* Imprint was designed to make the work of local writers accessible. This would help to stimulate thought and discussion in the community.

Open Hand published three more books under the *Littlebook* imprint: **Sistuh's Sermon on the Mount,** a collection of poems by Tamara Madison-Shaw; **Two Left Brains,** radio commentaries by Irv Pollack and George Holland, Jr.; and **The Babygetter_and other Homefolk Tales** by Randee Eddins, founder of the African American Writers Alliance in Seattle.

My assistant at the time, David Serra, and I designed the *Littlebooks*. Working with each of these authors was very satisfying. At the time I did not dream that this new form of publishing would become mainstream.

◊   ◊   ◊

Keeping up with frequent changes being made to computer programs was always a challenge. Each time the DacEasy accounting program was updated I had to learn how to use it all over again. Every few years technology changed to the point that our computer became obsolete and would have to be replaced by a more up-to-date one. At the end of each month a full day had to be devoted to reconciling and saving all of that month's transactions. It was a tedious task. At first they were saved onto floppy discs and after a few years "floppy discs" were replaced by "hard discs".

Ultimately "hard discs" were replaced by "CDs", whereas today everything is electronic and saved to the cloud.

◊ ◊ ◊

In spite of the miles that separated us, Jim Forman and I always reconciled after difficult periods and we remained close. We talked on the phone, if not daily, at least several times each week. For four or five years after moving to Seattle, I flew back to DC a couple of times each year to spend a week with him. It was always the same. Our happiness at being together would last for three days, then we would begin arguing about something trivial, and by the fifth day I couldn't wait to leave. When we were apart, our desire to be together never ceased in spite of our knowing this would happen. I felt like a moth being attracted to the light.

Three times Jim made the cross-country trip by train to Seattle. He didn't fly due to a problem he had with his ears. He enjoyed traveling by train as it reminded him of trips he had taken as a child from Chicago to visit his beloved grandmother in Mississippi.

In 1958 when I first met Jim, he was writing a novel called **The Song Festival**. Throughout the intense heat of Chicago's summer, he sat at the kitchen table in his mother's apartment typing the novel on an old portable typewriter. The story revolved around a friend who Jim had met at Roosevelt University, a young white preacher who had moved to Chicago from the South. Over the course of several years, as Jim worked on the novel, the story kept evolving to include more people, including a mixed-race couple. After Jim became involved with the civil rights movement and moved to Atlanta, the novel was lost, and Jim thought that it had been stolen. This distressed him a great deal. More than two decades passed and I do not know how or why, but the novel was returned to him. Jim wanted very much for Open Hand to publish it. He knew that it was incomplete and nowhere near ready for publication when he sent me a box with about 300 pages of manuscript, most of it the very same pages that I had watched him type back in Chicago 30 years earlier.

Knowing how much the story meant to Jim, I wanted very much to publish it. It was not coherent enough to hold together as a novel, but I thought it could be broken up into several short stories. This would require a great deal of editing and rewriting. Jim agreed, but said he didn't have time to work on it, so I asked Torie Scott if she would do the editing. In addition to the short stories, we added several speeches and essays: "Notes from Leflore County Jail," "The Invisible Struggle Against Racism, Colonialism, and Apartheid," "Colonial Territories and Colonized People." We called this book **High Tide of Black Resistance and other political & literary writings.** Jim would have preferred the title to be **The Song Festival**, but I thought that title would be more difficult to market. Perhaps I should have followed his advice. He was right about most things.

As a way of updating stories that Jim had written in the 1950s, I asked if he would write an introduction to each chapter. He wrote the introductions but his heart was not in it and they were short and not particularly informative. Nevertheless, the book is a reflection of his depth of thought and breath of interests. On the cover is a black and white photo, taken by another prisoner, of Jim in the Fort Payne, Alabama jail. The cover and book design was done by Holly Yasui. In addition to being an editor and designer, Holly is a writer and political activist with a clear understanding of the importance of the content of **High Tide of Black Resistance**. Working with her was a great pleasure.

◊   ◊   ◊

Jim and I often talked about writing a book together about our long relationship. We would have included the incident in late summer of 1958 when we spent a long weekend with friends in Buffalo. The presence of an interracial couple angered some neighbors to the point that they attempted to burn down the house in which we were staying. Fortunately, the woman who lived next door chased them away, removed the gasoline-soaked rags they had placed on the porch, and alerted us to what had happened. They had also let the air out of the tires of Jim's car and poured sugar into the gas tank. The car, although it was able to make the trip back to Chicago, was essentially destroyed.

◊ ◊ ◊

Ethelbert Miller made several trips to Seattle. On one of them he introduced me to Zoë Anglesey, a brilliant woman, worldly and sophisticated. Zoë was a long time resident of New York City, but had grown up in Centralia, a small town in Washington state. She moved easily between those two different worlds. Zoë had also lived in Central America and was editor of the bilingual anthology **Ixok Amar * Go: Central American Women's Poetry for Peace**. Zoë was looking for a place to stay in Seattle, and I offered her a room in my house. She stayed for several months before moving into a single room in an old neglected house one block north. In spite of never having enough money to pay for life's most basic necessities, Zoë was always full of enthusiasm. Almost everywhere she went she carried a wicker basket. Hidden away under cotton fabric were a tiny laptop computer and a printer, the size of a rolling pin. Zoë was always ready to write.

Five books were in production and all was going well for Open Hand when Zoë presented me with a manuscript for a bilingual anthology, *Stone on Stone: Poetry by Women of*

Diverse Heritages (Piedra Sobre Piedra: Poesia por mujeres de diversas culturas). It featured poetry by prize-winning women of diverse heritages within the United States to whom history and social concerns are of primary importance: Zoë, Mei Mei Berrse, Olga Broumas, Jayne Cortez, Sharon Doubiago, Rita Dove, Sandra Maria Esteves, Carolyn Forche, Tes Gallagher, Linda Gregg, Joy Harjo, Ntozake Shange, Anne Waldman, and C.D. Wright.

I never knew when I signed a contract with an author just how much or how little work would be required to prepare the book for production. Some flowed easily while others were exceedingly difficult and time consuming. This manuscript was complete when I received it and required no editing. Zoë had already obtained written permission for the use of each poem included in the anthology. Deb Figen designed the book and the cover.

◊ ◊ ◊

I had known Cindy Domingo ever since I moved to Seattle in 1978 and was a volunteer with *Crabshell Alliance*, trying to bring an end to nuclear power in the Northwest. Cindy worked at a neighborhood center called CAMP, short for the *Central Area Motivational Project. Crabshell* meetings were held there.

I received a phone call from Cindy in which she asked if she could come over with her sister-in-law, Terri Mast, and an author named Tom Churchill. They wanted to discuss a book proposal. We arranged for an evening meeting in my living room. Before this meeting, I knew nothing about the murder of Cindy's older brother Silme Domingo. He and Gene Viernes were assassinated in Seattle's Pioneer Square 13 years earlier, in 1981. Tom Churchill had written a novel based on the assassination and the trial that followed. Gene Viernes and Silme Domingo, Filipino-American cannery union organizers, were only twenty-nine at the time they were murdered. They had spent ten years reforming cannery workplaces where bosses and mob-related union foremen were highly resistant to change. Both college-educated activists, they angered many inside and outside the Filipino community because of their forceful, open fight for union reform and against the corruption that was taking place in the Philippines under the regime of Ferdinand Marcos. Immediately, I recognized this to be a very important story that I was eager to publish. The manuscript required minimal editing. Deb Figen designed the book and the cover. The only problem that arose was that the book had no title. A good title is essential if a book is to catch on and sell well. I wanted to call it **Murder in Seattle**, but my distributor's sales representatives knocked back the idea. We ended up calling the book **Triumph Over Marcos**, a reference to the final legal victory that went against Ferdinand Marcos. In spite of its receiving good reviews the book never sold well, and I attribute this, in part, to my not insisting on **Murder in Seattle**.

◊ ◊ ◊

Phyllis Hatfield was editing a book about how to become an entrepreneur, written by James Ujaama, a bright, idealistic, young black man. It was to be self-published. When Phyllis asked me if I would give James some tips about publishing, I agreed, and one morning James came over to my office. He was someone you wouldn't forget; polite, self-confident, and slightly aggressive. Still in his early twenties, James thought he was going to be somebody, and he wanted to help other young black entrepreneurs to succeed. He told me that both his father and his mother had been Black Panthers and were active in the civil rights movement in the 1960s and 70s.

Several months later I saw James at a community book fair where we were each exhibitors. His display table was across the aisle from mine. I greeted him and we shook hands. James introduced me to his brother, and when I held out my hand to him I was amazed and insulted when he said, "I don't shake hands with women." I could scarcely believe my ears.

Over the next few years, when James and I ran across one another in the community, he was always polite and friendly. It came as a shock in 2002 to learn that he had been arrested for conspiring to support al-Qaida, in part, by planning to build a terrorist training camp in Bly, Oregon. He was convicted of working with Abu Hamza al-Masri, the leader of a London mosque. According to the Seattle Post Intelligencer, April 15, 2003, Ujaama pleaded guilty and plea-bargained to cooperate fully regarding others engaged in criminal and terrorist activity. In exchange, he received a light 2-year prison sentence.

◊ ◊ ◊

In November of 1990, I attended the first conference of the Multicultural Publishers' Exchange (MPE) held in Madison, Wisconsin. As a white woman publishing books about African American issues, I sometimes encountered distain from whites who thought it was not an appropriate subject, and resentment from blacks who thought I was interfering in their affairs. So when I walked into a largely black conference of writers and publishers to speak about **The Black West,** I had no idea how I would be received. As it turned out the majority of the people at the conference were glad to learn about the book and the publishing company. It was a pleasant surprise when a woman came up to me and said, "You were brave to come in and stand up in front of this crowd."

At the end of the conference, I was nominated and elected to be on the Board of the organization. Black nationalists that were present didn't show up when we met the following year.

◊ ◊ ◊

Having acquired the Talman Company as our distributor, and having published two new books, **Black Heroes of the Wild West** and **Love, Debra,** I felt, as 1990 came to an end, that much progress was being made. Open Hand was receiving a lot of support and publicity in Seattle with long articles about it appearing in the *Seattle Weekly, Elliott Bay Booknotes,* and the *Capitol Hill Times.*

Talman received an order from Barnes & Noble for 800 copies **of Puerto Rican Writers at Home in the USA.** This was the largest order for any single title that I had ever received. Little did I know that within a few months Barnes & Noble would return 700. Bookstores are always allowed returns. You might say the book business is done on a consignment basis. Prior to this, returns from independent bookstores had not been a big problem. Small publishing companies like Open Hand were not equipped to deal with the unpredictability resulting from sales to chain bookstores like Barnes & Noble, and Borders.

Also, new on the scene was Amazon, which in the beginning only sold books. This newly established business was located about three miles from my house. When the first order came in from Amazon, I thought, great. I can deliver the order by hand, like I do with the other bookstores in Seattle. NOT SO. There was no place in the Amazon building where one could leave a package. I have frequently been asked, "Was Amazon damaging to Open Hand in the way that Barnes & Noble and Borders were?" It wasn't. Amazon always paid promptly and there were no returns. It was a good customer.

A huge shift was taking place in the book industry. Independent bookstores were going out of business all across the United States because they could not price books as low as the new chain bookstores, Borders, and Barnes & Noble. Within about three years more than three quarters of the independent bookstores in the United States were forced to close their doors. Even the largest and strongest independent bookstores were struggling to survive.

Bookstores were unable to pay distributors, distributors then could not pay publishers, so publishers could not pay royalty to their authors. The whole industry was collapsing like dominos. Somehow, it didn't occur to me that this might be a good time to get out of the business. Instead, I turned to using credit cards to keep the bills paid. I phoned Marilee Talman almost daily asking when I could expect the $40,000. owing to Open Hand. She stopped accepting my calls. I was fortunate that before Talman went out of business they sent me a check for half that was owed. Other publishers received less.

Amidst all this drama Bill Katz had an offer from Simon and Schuster to publish **The Black West,** and he wanted the rights to that book returned to him. Terrified of losing Open Hand's best selling title, I refused. Katz, in turn, sued Open Hand. The argument between us went on for over a year. I counted on that book to keep Open Hand afloat and did not see how we could survive without it. If I recall correctly, we usually did a print run of 5,000 paperback copies and they would last about a year. When the stock became low we would have more printed. I entered into a long, bitter, energy consuming legal battle with Bill Katz for which I was ill equipped. Communication was largely through our lawyers. Fortunately, I had a friend, Richard Reinhardt, who was a lawyer and who charged me very little for his services. Richard was an angel. We had known one another since 1979, shortly after the disaster at Thee

119

Mile Island, when we were each members of Crabshell Alliance working to stop nuclear power. Ultimately, I lost the rights to **The Black West**, and I was required to pay Bill Katz $17,000. for his legal fees. It is difficult to imagine now what motivated me to keep on publishing. I was so deeply into it that I didn't stop to think of another role for myself. I still thought that if I could just keep going things would eventually turn out well. I was committed to making Open Hand successful and never doubted that it would be anything else. I saw hope in each new title and always kept an eye out for "the book" that everybody would want to read. I had learned how to produce beautiful, high quality, award-winning books, and get them reviewed in leading national publications.

◊   ◊   ◊

The local press continued to give Open Hand very good coverage. Articles about the press appeared in the *Seattle Weekly*, and the *Capitol Hill Times* and *Elliott Bay Book Notes*. Jerry Large, a reporter from the *Seattle Times* came to my office to interview me for an article that was published on June 9, 1996. I was surprised when I read his opening sentence: *"I didn't tell Anna this, but when I rang the doorbell of her Capitol Hill home, I expected to be greeted by a middle-aged black woman."*

◊   ◊   ◊

The production of each book had its own rhythm. While some were a delight to work on, others were like pulling teeth. I was delighted to sign a book contract for an autobiography by a woman of mixed African American and Native American heritage. She had a fascinating story, although it was still largely unwritten. Over time, it became apparent that the manuscript would require a great deal of editing. I hired an excellent editor, Deborah Kaufmann, to edit the book. We had worked together before on **Triumph over Marcos** and I was looking forward to the collaboration. Tragically, Deborah learned that she had an inoperable cancerous growth on her pancreas and had only a few months to live. This, however, did not prevent her from continuing with the book project. The author came to Seattle and we went together to Deborah's hospital room where we all worked on the manuscript together.

Weeks passed with Deborah and the author passing the manuscript back and forth. All of the editing this book required was an added expense that I had not anticipated. In the meantime, I was writing promotional material about the book – meeting the deadlines and demands of my distributor. Promotion of a book begins at least 6 months prior to its being printed. I was caught completely off guard when I received a phone call from the author in which she told me, "I'm not going through with the book. I don't want it published." There was nothing I could do. Not only was I out several thousand dollars, but in order to meet my commitment to my distributor, I needed to come up fast with another title. Also, I had to meet an obligation to the National Endowment for the Arts who had given Open Hand a $12,000 grant to assist with the publication of a literary work.

Pat Andrus, my friend, as well as manuscript editor, and I had never discussed publishing her poetry, although I knew that some of her poems had appeared in national literary publications. On a hunch that there might be a book there, I phoned Pat, explained the situation, and asked if she was prepared to publish a book with Open Hand. She did indeed have a body of poems she wanted published. My problem was solved. Thus, **Old Woman of Irish Blood** came into being. Poet, Christine Balk says, "**Old Woman** resounds as an outcry of reverence, encouraging us to embrace...birth as well as growth, death as well as rebirth. By pushing beyond our modern fascination with youth, her poems allow us to coexist with the natural world..."

◊ ◊ ◊

Danny Peck, my friend from Washington, DC, told Louise Meyer about Open Hand's multicultural books. Louise approached me about publishing a photographic children's book about a master weaver from Ghana. The color photos by Nestor Hernandez were spectacular. I knew it would be a wonderful book and I decided to publish it in hard back. Deb Figen did a magnificent job of designing the book and the cover. Both educational and beautiful, **Master Weaver from Ghana** received the "1998 Notable Books for Children" award from the Smithsonian Institution, the "1999 Notable Social Studies Trade Books for Young People" award from the Children's Book Council and the National Council for Social Studies, as well as the "1999 Best Book for Young Children" award from the African Studies Association.

Regrettably, this came too late, as we no longer had good distribution. After the Talman Company went bankrupt, there were not a lot of options. Knowing that all the distribution companies were in trouble, I decided to go with a small distribution company in Oregon called Subterranean owned by Craig and Claudia Broadley. They distributed for City Lights Books in San Francisco. They were honest people trying to do their best but they did not have experienced sales reps that understood the children's book market. We kept limping along from month to month.

During this difficult period I thought it was important to maintain high standards for the editing and design of each book. I had the good fortune to find a highly skilled editor, Pat Welch. Working with her was a pleasure. It was a surprise to learn that her son and his young family lived across the street from me.

◊　◊　◊

Throughout the 1990s, I had made frequent trips back to DC to visit Jim. He had such a one-track mind on work; it was a pleasant surprise to see a beautiful philodendron in his apartment. He took very excellent care of it always making sure that it had enough water and light. The plant responded well and grew so tall that it almost touched the ceiling. It was a delight to see Jim taking so much pleasure in cultivating a plant, an entirely new experience for him.

◊　◊　◊

It was a disappointment when the building downtown in Pioneer Square in which Open Hand's office was located was sold and we were forced to relocate. The new owners had other ideas for the space. After looking at several office spaces, I decided to move the operation back into my home. Just around this time my assistant, Torie Scott, was accepted into graduate school at the University of Washington and I was without an assistant. I phoned the office of the Multicultural Publisher's Exchange (MPE) in Madison to ask if they knew of anyone who might be interested in the job. David Serra, who I knew from MPE conferences, answered the phone and the conversation went something like this:

> Anna: I am looking for a publisher's assistant and wonder if you know of anyone who might be interested.
> David: Yes! I am! When does the job begin?
> Anna: On Monday.
> David: I'll be there!

And he was. Once again I was exceedingly fortunate to find an assistant who was capable, eager to take on responsibility, and also companionable.

◊ ◊ ◊

Manuscripts kept arriving in the mail and I continued to be approached by authors wanting their book published. If Open Hand was to remain viable it had to produce new titles each year. Mona Lee, a long-time Seattle peace activist, asked me if I would read her manuscript and consider it for publication. I was charmed by the story set in the beautiful San Juan Islands about an alien visitor from a more evolved planet where there is no war. It is an important cautionary tale that calls into scrutiny mainstream American war culture. Although science fiction, it seemed to fit well with Open Hand's books calling for a peaceful and just world.

The only way I could afford to publish books at this point was if the author was to pay for the design and printing. I didn't like doing this as it was too much like vanity publishing in which authors pay to have their books published and there is no criteria for the selection of books, whereas the traditional publisher sets a standard and takes a financial risk on each book. Publishing companies do not break even on most books: but the successful books make enough to enable the company to keep going. Mona Lee was more than happy to pay for production costs. And thus came into existence Open Hand's first science fiction book, **Alien Child**.

◊ ◊ ◊

The last book I published was **Forged by the Knife: The Experience of Surgical Residency from the Perspective**

of a Woman of Color. Patricia Dawson, M.D., PhD., FACS, was a leading breast surgeon in Seattle. Publishing her book was an honor. Little editing was required. Deb Figen designed the book and the cover. I always enjoyed working with Deb on ideas for book covers. At first, this cover presented something of a challenge. It had to be a knife. Not wanting it to be too graphic, I asked the author for a surgical knife that I took to my friend Susan Russell, artist and calligrapher, and asked her for a drawing of the knife. Deb was able to put it all together in a way that made for an attractive and appropriate cover.

Forged by the Knife received excellent reviews. Former Surgeon General of the United States, M. Joycelyn Elders, M.D., said, "This is an insightful look into the making of Black female surgeons and the long, rigorous hours of the surgical residency. The reader can feel the pain, isolation, and loneliness of being excluded – while still having to bear the responsibility of making life-and-death decisions, with someone watching over your shoulder."

This book should have sold well across the country but, unfortunately, our distribution system was weak at this time. As always, Seattle's University of Washington Bookstore and Elliott Bay Books continued purchasing Open Hand's books, even though they too were struggling to survive. University bookstores across the country were being bought out by Barnes & Noble. For a long time my mind remained in suspended disbelief about the collapse of the book industry.

◊　◊　◊

My dear friend, Carol Hoyt, invited me to join a group of women called the *Raging Grannies* who were coming together to sing political satire. When I said: I'm not a grandmother, and I can't sing." Carol replied, "It doesn't matter."

So, we joined about 10 other women in a rehearsal for the *Seattle Raging Grannies* debut performance on February 12, 1996, in Olympia, Washington. Decked out in outrageous hats and colorful granny costumes we assembled in the pouring rain on the Capitol steps for a Presidents' Day rally sponsored by the Washington State Labor Council. We began with our theme song, *Oh, We are a Gaggle of Grannies* and ended with *No More War!*

The *Raging Grannies* originated in 1987 in British Columbia when activists came together to protest the presence of US nuclear submarines in Canadian waters. It was not long before more than 25 *gaggles of Grannies* sprung up all across Canada. Each group changed the words of familiar tunes to suit their particular circumstances.

The *Seattle Raging Grannies* practiced regularly and performed several times each month before both small audiences and massive crowds. We sang and spoke about the environment, military spending, racism, women's rights, and a host of other social concerns.

At the end of November 1999, *Canadian Raging Grannies* came to Seattle and joined with the *Seattle Raging Grannies* as we protested the World Trade Organization (WTO). There were tanks in the streets and teargas in the air as hundreds of demonstrators were arrested. After performing in a church, we marched with dozens of others to the downtown public library where we stood silently in the street witnessing the violence being inflicted upon our city. Our silent witness went on for over an hour as soldiers in an armored tank watched over us from the opposite side of the intersection. We wondered if we would be sprayed with teargas or run over. Finally, someone began to quietly hum *We Shall Overcome* and gradually everyone joined in. It took courage to stand before that tank and the police and it was not something I could have done alone.

As a result of the WTO the *Raging Grannies* received worldwide media attention. Our movement began to grow rapidly all across the US and in other parts of the world. This growth was helped greatly when my son, Jorma, created a web page www.raginggrannies.com. (Last I looked it was still up and going strong.) He had just graduated from UC Santa Cruz and was working for an early web provider, web.com. The web was just coming into existence, and when he said to me, "Mom, I want to build Open Hand a web page." I replied, "What's that?" After he explained it to me, it sounded like more than I wanted to deal with, so I said, "Thanks, but I don't want one." Not wanting to disappoint him, I said, "Maybe you could build one for the Raging Grannies." I had no idea what a web page was. It took a year or so before I began to see the benefits. Jorma also built a beautiful website for Open Hand before they became commonplace.

◊ ◊ ◊

Difficult as things were, I remained determined that Open Hand was going to be successful. So many things had gone wrong; losing our best selling title, **The Black West,** being owed money by the Talman Company when they went out of business, and having to move from the Pioneer Square office. Things had not worked out well with Subterranean, our new distributor, so we went back to distributing the books ourselves. My wonderful assistant, David Serra handled most of the fulfillment and packing of books. The FAX (short for *facsimile*) machine was just invented. With it I sent and received scanned printed material via my telephone, connected to a printer. It seemed like magic. Now orders arrived seconds after they had been placed, instead of the three to five days that it took them to travel by ordinary mail, which people were then coming to refer to as *snail mail.* FAXes were printed on cheap shiny paper that had a short life. The ink faded quickly so correspondence that arrived by FAX became illegible after a few months. My bedroom was located directly above the Open Hand office and many mornings I was awakened before 6 AM by the grinding of the FAX machine. . It was satisfying to know that orders were arriving from the East coast, which was three hours ahead of Seattle.

I struggled desperately to hold on as everything grew worse. There were weeks when I scarcely had enough money to buy food. The only income I had was from renting rooms in my house, and that was not enough to keep the bills paid. I started earning a little money by helping Pat Andrus with a housekeeping job she had. Then, it occurred to me that by doing gardening I could earn about fourteen dollars per hour. It was springtime and I had always enjoyed gardening. BUT, I didn't know how to start. I didn't know how to find customers and negotiate with them. When I told my friend Thurman Holmes about my idea, he volunteered to help me get started by going with me to the first job. Thurman suggested I post a 3 x 5 card in the neighborhood health food store advertising my availability. I did as he suggested! And within a few hours I received phone calls from people who were looking for someone to help them with their overrun garden. Thurman and I both went to that first job, and from then on I was on my own and quite enjoying my new occupation. For two summers, I worked at my desk in the Open Hand office in the morning and did gardening in the afternoon.

While the bookstore market had fallen apart, orders from libraries remained steady. Also, some of our books were being used as texts by university professors. **Puerto Rican Writers at Home in the USA** was popular among English teachers. Julian Bond placed **The Making of Black Revolutionaries** on the required reading list for each of his students in the history department at the University of

Virginia. He taught over 100 students each semester and orders for those books went a long way towards helping to sustain Open Hand during a difficult period.

I continued to believe that sales would improve, that we would receive an option for a movie based on one of our titles, or that some miracle would happen. I also began to explore various other alternatives. Sandy Taylor, publisher of Curbstone Press who I had come to know at the Nicaraguan Book Festival, urged me to make Open Hand into a non-profit organization. Many small literary presses are organized that way. Having been on the Boards of several non-profit organizations, I knew it would entail forming a Board to which I would become answerable. I was not interested in going that route.

Several people suggested that Open Hand declare bankruptcy, which would mean closing the company and leaving its debts unpaid. I felt a strong responsibility for paying of all my debts and never gave a second thought to declaring bankruptcy.

◊ ◊ ◊

I was fortunate to have David Serra as my assistant during the difficult final years. Extremely capable and reliable, David had a way of putting people at ease. He screened the phone calls and gracefully handled those people who were disgruntled, rather than passing them along to me. I regretted not being able to raise his salary. I was sad, but not too surprised, when he resigned in order to take a better paying job with a computer game company. I did not hire another assistant after David left.

For a long time I had resisted any thought that Open Hand might not succeed. I loved my work and thought it was valuable. My hope was always pinned on the next book – that it would be a great success. Then, one day the realization came to me that I had become addicted to gambling, always gambling on the next book. Knowing this was an unhealthy situation that must come to an end, I finally made the decision to sell Open Hand.

The first thing I did was to phone Jim and tell him that I could no longer go on with Open Hand and that I was going to attempt to sell the company. He asked to have the rights to his books returned to him. Without hesitation, I agreed. He purchased the remaining inventory of his four books at a price that covered their production cost. I boxed up the files that contained all correspondence about each book and sent them to him. This correspondence now resides in the James Forman Collection at the Library of Congress.

I let it be known, primarily by word of mouth, that Open Hand was for sale. The authors were the first to be told. With the exception of Jim, they all left their titles with Open Hand. Then, I contacted other publishers. I had been a Board member of *Publishers Northwest* since 1988, along with Pat Snowdon, publisher of the University of Washington Press. I was thrilled when Pat told me that he wanted to purchase the Rights to **The Making of Black Revolutionaries.** Jim was pleased with this arrangement.

After I stopped accepting manuscripts and publishing new titles, there was a lot more time to devote to activist activities with *Seattle Women Act for Peace* (SWAP) and the *Seattle Raging Grannies.*

It came as a surprise when one of the Raging Grannies, Kathleen Kelley, told me that her son-in-law, Richard Koritz was interested in purchasing Open Hand. Richard, a postal worker and union organizer in Greensboro, North Carolina was about to retire. When he made a trip to Seattle to discuss the purchase of Open Hand, I could see he was enthusiastic about the prospect of beginning a new career as a publisher. Each of Open Hand's authors agreed to the sale. In June of 2000, Richard made me an offer.

Sunday June 4, 2000

When I went down stairs this morning there was a FAX letter from Richard Koritz offering $52,000 for the purchase of Open Hand. I could just accept his offer and sell immediately. But there is a woman in New Mexico who is also interested. She saw my ad in The Weekly. I'm going to go a little slow.

I agonized for a couple of months about the sale of Open Hand.

Sunday, July 30, 2000

My favorite month almost at an end. August is just as nice, plus peaches will be in season – but in August one knows summer is half over, and you no longer can pretend it will go on and on.

So, last Thursday night I finally made up my mind, and on Friday I phoned Richard Koritz to let him know that if he is still interested, Open Hand is available to him. YES. He's still interested and wants the transition to go through as soon as possible. I'm thrilled. I can't wait. Will try to talk with a lawyer to draw up the papers ASAP.

Monday, August 14, 2000

Holy shit – what a day!

I've been sitting on tenderhooks for more than a week waiting to hear from Richard Koritz about his purchasing Open Hand. He has been very clear that he wtnts to buy it for $52,000 but I'm not going to really believe it or celebrate until the contract has been signed on the dotted line and I have a check in my hand.

Tonight I received a phone call from him confirming his intention to buy and agreeing to immediately send me a deposit of $1,000. So I guess it's for real ... it must be for real. He, his daughter, Rachel, and a friend who will be a co-owner plan to come to Seattle in mid-September to finalize everything – to pack up the books and the files, etc., and to take them away. My burden will be lifted.

Tuesday, September 14, 2000

... I'm finally allowing myself to think that, yes, it really does look as though they will buy the company. Papers will be signed and we'll pack everything up, and it will all be shipped away. The basement will be empty. The little meditation room will be empty. The office suite will be empty. The business phone will be disconnected. The FAX machine will be disconnected. I won't be going each day to the post office on my bicycle. My, my, my, my, my! What will life be like?

Thursday, September 18, 2000

I'm exhausted. Richard Koritz, Melissa Dimunstein, and Richard's daughter, Rachel, arrived last Thursday and it was a very fast, very intense crash course on publishing, plus office administration, plus packing of books ----- all leading up to Richard and I signing the contract in Mark Vohr's office this afternoon. I never would have dreamed that the legal proceedings would be so complex and would require so much time. But, we finally signed, and Richard handed me a check for $51,000.

The funny thing is that when I came home, I didn't feel any different. I don't really have any feeling about it at all. Maybe because I'm so exhausted. I did phone Jorma and we talked about how great it is. Arlo wasn't in, so I left a message on his answering machine.

The most enjoyable part of the sale activities was yesterday afternoon when I held a "Drop In" for the authors to meet the new publisher. It was from 3 - 6, but it went on 'til 8 o'clock. Tom Churchill (**Triumph Over Marcos**) came first. He was followed by Pat Andrus (**Old Woman of Irish Blood**), then Mona Lee (**Alien Child**); and they were all here at the same time. Then Carletta Wilson (**Nightfeathers** and **Habari Gani? What's the News?**) arrived, and she was overlapped by LaVerne and Mahji Hall ("**T**" **is for** "**Terrific**/ "**T es por** "**Terrifico**"). Carletta stayed on when Pat Dawson (**Forged by the Knife**) arrived. All the while, we sat on the back deck - on a warm and lovely late summer day. Pat Andrus, at Mona Lee's prompting, did a reading from her book. Richard and Melissa were delighted by the experience.

Today is a day of convergence. Not only did I sell Open Hand, but my first social security check arrived.

Sunday, September 24, 2000

Earlier in the week I asked Arlo and Jorma about suggestions for how we should celebrate the sale of Open Hand. Arlo phoned tonight saying he and Jorma had talked about it, and how about meeting at Jorma's (in Santa Cruz) and going for a kayak trip. I can't think of anything more wonderful.

Post Script

M uch changed as a result of selling Open Hand, but much remained the same. Jim and I continued to communicate, work jointly for social change, and generally support one another. I organized a rally in front of the Federal Building in Seattle at which the Seattle Raging Grannies called for statehood for the District of Columbia, a major focus of Jim's. We spent five weeks together just before he died of cancer in the winter of 2005.

◊ ◊ ◊

On August 9, 2001, Nagasaki Day, I was arrested along with nine other peace activists, for stepping over the line onto the Naval Submarine Base at Bangor, Silverdale, Washington. Charges were never pressed and we did not have to appear in court.

◊ ◊ ◊

Early in the morning on September 11th 2001, I was in the kitchen preparing breakfast when the phone rang. It was my sister, Bess who said in an urgent voice, "Turn on your TV". And when I did I saw the video that is now all so familiar – of a plane flying into the twin towers in New York City. My sister's entire family was in lower Manhattan that day and she had not heard from them.

Unable to comprehend what was happening, let alone explain it to the two young Japanese students who were staying with me, I simply said to them, "You must watch the TV." They, of course, were confused and frightened. It was a relief when the University of Washington gathered all the students in the language program together and had them stay in a dormitory. They were unable to return to Japan on schedule because for three days all of the planes in the United States were grounded. It was so silent with no planes overhead.

By the end of the day I learned that everyone in my sister's family was OK. Thousands of Seattleites brought flowers from their gardens to the Seattle Center. Everyone was silent and many were in tears as we stood in a procession waiting to place our flowers in a huge circle. This is the only time I have seen grown men crying openly. There was a powerful feeling of tragedy and unity, and absolutely no notion of revenge among the vast throng of people. The mood was one of solemnity and beauty.

◊ ◊ ◊

July 2002 was the beginning of a new chapter in my life. I moved to Portland, Oregon where I rented an apartment not far from Torie Scott, Ernie Jones and their two-year-old son, Roland. Comfortably settled in my new apartment, I set about writing a memoir, **Australia Years: the Life of a Nuclear Migrant** published in 2005.

-END-

Appendix

Books Published by Open Hand Publishing Inc.

© date	Title	Author
1981	Self-Determination: An Examination of the Question and its Application to the African-American People	James Forman Ph.D.
1982	Little Bitty Snake / La Vibora Chiquilina	Jorma Rodieck
1982	Little Bitty Snake / Le Tout P'tit Serpent	Jorma Rodieck
1982	Little Bitty Snake / Chisana Chisana Hebi	Jorma Rodieck
1985	The Making of Black Revolutionaries	James Forman Ph.D.
1986	Sammy Youge: Jr.: The First Black College Student to Die in the Black Liberation Movement.	James Forman Ph.D.
1986	Where are the Love Poems for Dictators?	E. Ethelbert Miller
1986	The Invisible Empire: The Ku Klux Klan Impact on History	William Loren Katz
1987	The Black West	William Loren Katz
1989	Surviving the Fire: Mother Courage & World War II	Lilo Kluge

© date	Title	Author
1989	Mississippi to Madrid: Memoir of a Black American in the Abraham Lincoln Brigade	James Yates
1989	Nightfeathers	Sundaira Morninghouse
1989	"T" is for "Terrific" / "T" es por "terrifico"	Mahji Hall
1990	Love, Debra	Fritz Hamilton
1990	Black Heroes of the Wild West	Ruth Pelz
1991	Puerto Rican Writers at Home in the USA	Faythe Turner, editor
1991	Sylvia Stark: A Pioneer	Victoria Scott & Ernest Jones
1992	Everybody Has Feelings / Todos tenemos sentimientos: The Moods of Children	Charles Avery
1992	Habari Gani: What's the News?	Sundaira Morninghouse
1992	Pathblazers: Eight People Who Made a Difference	M.K. Fullen
1993	Nailing Hammering Man (Littlebook)	Selma Waldman
1993	Sistuh's Sermon on the Mount (Littlebook)	Tamara Madison-Shaw
1994	Two Left Brains (Littlebook)	Irv Pollack & George Howland, Jr.
1994	The Baby Getter (Littlebook)	Randee Eddins
1994	High Tide of Black Resistance and Other Literary Political Writings	James Forman, Ph.D.

© date	Title	Author
1994	Stone on Stone / Piedra sobre piedra Poetry by Women of Diverse Heritages / Poesia por mujeres de diversas culturas	Zoë Anglesey
1994	Contribution Series Curriculum Guides	
1995	Women of the Wild West	Ruth Pelz
1995	Triumph over Marcos	Tom Churchill
1996	Old Woman of Irish Blood	Pat Andrus
1998	Master Weaver from Ghana	Gilbert "Bobbo" Ahiagble & Louise Meyer
1999	Alien Child	Mona Lee
1999	Forged by the Knife: The Experience of Surgical Residency from the Perspective Of a Woman of Color	Patricia L. Dawson, M.D. Ph.D., FACS